Writing the Multicul

"This is an important and timely textbook for teachers and students of Creative Writing who would like to bring a strong multicultural approach and experience to all aspects of their workshop practice. It's full of excellent practical advice, writing exercises and references. A much needed addition to the field of Creative Writing teaching and pedagogy."

—Ardashir Vakil, *Senior Lecturer in Creative Writing, Goldsmiths College, University of London, UK*

Pauline Kaldas

Writing the Multicultural Experience

palgrave
macmillan

Pauline Kaldas
Hollins University, Roanoke, VA, USA

ISBN 978-3-031-06123-3   ISBN 978-3-031-06124-0   (eBook)
https://doi.org/10.1007/978-3-031-06124-0

This Palgrave Macmillan imprint is published by the registered company Springer Nature Switzerland AG.
The registered company address is: Gewerbestrasse 11, 6330 Cham, Switzerland

To my students

Acknowledgments

I am grateful for the support I have received as a faculty member at Hollins University. Having the freedom to design my own courses and develop my style as a teacher led to the writing of this book. Special thanks to the Hollins University Wyndham Robertson Library Retreat, where I first began this project.

My appreciation goes to Molly Beck at Palgrave Macmillan who reviewed the first draft of this manuscript and guided me through a process of revision that enhanced and improved the book. Additional thanks goes to Imogen Higgins for her excellent help with the preparation of the manuscript.

I am eternally indebted to my friend, Lisa Suhair Majaj, who introduced me to Arab American literature, putting me on the path to becoming a writer and teacher of multicultural literature.

My sincere thanks goes to Marcia Douglas, who first gave me the idea for this class.

I am forever grateful to my husband, T.J. Anderson III, who is also my colleague at Hollins University. We have taken this journey of teaching together and he remains one of my greatest mentors.

My heartfelt appreciation goes to my daughters, Yasmine and Celine, who watched me all those years preparing for classes, grading papers, and coming up with new assignments. They have both become extraordinary teachers, and their support and suggestions for this book have been invaluable.

My deep thanks to Yad Jabbarpour who encouraged this project and kept urging me to complete it.

And to my students at Hollins University, who have traveled through each class with me and taught me so much.

Contents

About the Author

Pauline Kaldas is the author of *Looking Both Ways, The Time Between Places, Letters from Cairo*, and *Egyptian Compass*. She also co-edited *Dinarzad's Children: An Anthology of Contemporary Arab American Fiction* and *Beyond Memory: An Anthology of Contemporary Arab American Creative Nonfiction*. She was awarded a fellowship in fiction from the Virginia Commission for the Arts and has been in residency at MacDowell, the Virginia Center for the Creative Arts, the Writer's Colony at Dairy Hollow, and Green Olive Arts in Tetouan, Morocco. She is Professor of English and Creative Writing at Hollins University, USA.

A Diverse Approach to Teaching Creative Writing

Over the past two decades, there has been a proliferation of graduate creative writing programs as well as undergraduate creative writing departments and majors. Alongside, the number of creative writing textbooks has multiplied. Inevitably, the question is why another one? Most of these books speak to a general audience. In doing so, little if any attention is paid to the issues that concern multicultural writers. At the beginning of the Introduction to her book, *How Dare We! Write*, Sherry Quan Lee asks, "Where are the textbooks by writers of color whose work has been/is being silenced, ignored, and recklessly criticized; writers who have been vocally undermined, or on the other hand, patronized" (i). This book is an attempt to respond to that question by speaking to the needs of multicultural writers.

Despite the rise of multicultural literature in the U.S. and the number of young diverse writers in college today, most of the current creative writing books are inadequate in addressing the needs of writers of color and other diverse writers. This is perhaps a reflection of the fact that multicultural literature has not entered most creative writing classrooms. Much has been recently written about the whiteness of creative writing programs. See Junot Diaz's "MFA vs. POC" in *The New Yorker*, David Mura's "Ferguson, Whiteness as Default and the Teaching of Creative Writing," Claudia Rankin's "In Our Way: Racism in Creative Writing," and Fred D'Aguiar's "Toward A New Creative Writing Pedagogy," all in *The Writer's Chronicle*. These articles highlight the embedded racism within the structure of creative writing programs as well as the damage it does to writers of color.

We need a different approach to teaching creative writing, one that is inclusive and centers the concerns of multicultural writers rather than abandoning

P. Kaldas, *Writing the Multicultural Experience*,
https://doi.org/10.1007/978-3-031-06124-0_1

or pushing them to the periphery. From the beginning, the U.S. was a multi-cultural nation, and writing by diverse people has always been present. The nature of American identity remains a constant battle—those who colonized the U.S. strived for a homogenous society while stealing land from Indigenous Peoples and enslaving Africans for the use of their labor. A homogeneous national identity was impossible from the moment that Columbus brutalized this land. Thomas Jefferson struggled with how to achieve this vision of a homogeneous society. His solution for eliminating enslaved people was to separate the children from their parents and, once old enough, to take them to Santo Domingo, while "the old stock would die off in the ordinary course of nature, lessening from the commencement until its final disappearance" (qtd. in Takaki 45). In the case of Native Americans, Jefferson advocated either assimilation or elimination. As Takaki explains, "His two views—civilization and extermination—were not contradictory: They were both consistent with his vision of a 'homogeneous' American society" (55). Similarly, Jefferson wanted to keep out immigrants who would dilute the purity of the American nation. Jefferson's vision for the nation failed, yet it makes apparent the systemic racism that has existed since the founding of the U.S. Today, our diversity is what gives our nation strength. With the abundance of multicultural writers and the racial concerns under scrutiny in our country, it is time to re-center the creative writing classroom around those issues that relate to diversity.

A Journey Toward Writing

Having immigrated from Egypt at the age of eight, I arrived in the U.S. at the end of 1969 to find a segregated America with little understanding of diversity. My family came two years after the 1965 Immigration and Naturalization Act was passed. If it were not for this act, we would not have been able to come to the U.S. In 1924, an immigration act was passed, one of the most evident examples of the attempt to create a homogeneous society. Using the quota system, the majority of immigrants allowed to enter the country were to come from Western Europe while only a few were permitted from other parts of the world, such as Africa, the Middle East, Asia, and Eastern Europe. Alongside the 1924 Act, several other acts were implemented to limit or inhibit immigration, such as the Chinese Exclusion Act in 1882 and the Gentleman's Agreement with Japan in 1907.

The 1965 Act repealed the 1924 Immigration Act, enabling people to come from those countries where immigration had been restricted. This was in part fueled by a need for professional labor. My father's profession as an Engineer was a major factor in our acceptance for immigration by the U.S. However, in 1969, most people had never met anyone from Egypt and what little my classmates knew was based on the ancient Egypt they studied in History, leading them to ask me if I owned a camel and if I had lived in the pyramids.

The English language school I attended in Egypt, The Ramses College for Girls, had not prepared me for the slang of American English. My teachers were British women who spoke with crisp pronunciation and clear diction. They pronounced their words precisely, articulating each letter. Whether that was their natural speaking pattern or whether they did it for the benefit of the Egyptian girls whom they taught, I cannot be sure. But once in America, the words people spoke sounded garbled to my ear as if they had gone through a blender before being uttered. For the first six months, I understood nothing, and I retreated into silence.

The first school I attended in the U.S. was St. Peter's School in Cambridge, Massachusetts. After I had been there for six months, my parents received the letter telling them I would need to repeat the fourth grade. The following year, words began to have meaning. I had spent the summer in front of our new television, and the sounds untangled and made words. It was during that second year of fourth grade that our class went to the local small library, and my teacher pointed me to the fairytale books, perhaps thinking they would match my reading level. At night, I would hold a flashlight under the covers and keep reading about kings and queens, princesses and knights, and their adventures. The stories ignited my imagination as they took place in another world, outside the constraints of either America or Egypt. And they inspired in me the desire to create my own stories.

In college, I took the creative writing classes offered by the visiting writers. My early attempts at poetry were encouraged by Carol Oles, who was perhaps the first person to recognize the subject of my writing. I had written a few poems based on my memories of growing up in Egypt, and she suggested I write a series of such poems. That suggestion remained with me even though it was often clouded by other influences. I struggled through other creative writing classes where my attempts at writing about being Egyptian in America were received with either indifference or lack of understanding. By the time I graduated in 1983, I had concluded that no one would want to read the stories I wrote, that there was no place for them in this new world.

It would take a long time for me to believe that my writing had value. And it would take longer to believe that I had the right to call myself a writer. My husband, T. J. Anderson III, an African American poet whom I met while we were both graduate students at the University of Michigan, helped to bring me back to my writing. And my deep friendship, also at the University of Michigan, with the writer and scholar, Lisa Suhair Majaj, showed me that there was a history and a community for Arab American writers. The three years I spent teaching at the American University in Cairo reminded me that the world I came from had relevance with stories that deserved to be told, and my time as a PhD student at Binghamton University, especially my friendship with the writer Marcia Douglas from Jamaica, showed me that there were other writers like me.

Having attended college and graduate school in the 1980s and 1990s, my education offered little diversity in either literature or creative writing classes. As a writer of color, I never found a place for my work within the classroom. My peers required things I was not willing or interested in providing—often these centered on notions of the exotic. While I wanted to explore what it meant to have left my homeland and to have re-created myself in this new country—culture, identity, family, language—all those things that give us a sense of self, my audience desired an exotic fantasy land. Even today, Egypt remains a place associated with the mystical and the ancient. The Egypt of my experience was not the one that existed in people's minds. At times, it seemed that readers wanted a tourist brochure rather than a work of literature. Other times, the request seemed to be for an anthropological text, one that would explain the culture to them. I wanted to tell stories about people and their lives. No one talked about language, exoticism, or audience expectations in any of the classes I took. In his book, *A Stranger's Journey: Race, Identity, and Narrative Craft in Writing*, David Mura says, "We know we cannot fully describe the experiences of our lives without reference to race, without employing the lens of race" (24). Most classrooms make little room for this lens, instead relegating race to the periphery, using terms such as universal appeal to indicate that race should not be centered in a writer's work. It was a long process of trial and error and discovery to sort through my specific concerns. What I wish is that there had been a class that addressed what mattered to me as writer.

Teaching

I have been teaching for over thirty years. For the past twenty-three years, I have been at Hollins University, teaching both literature and creative writing courses. My literature courses include Immigrant Literature, Arab American Literature, Multicultural Women Writers, International Women's Voices, Arab Women Writers, and Multicultural Children's Literature. The diversity in literature curriculums came about as a result of the hard work of students and faculty who have challenged and continue to challenge the white-dominated curriculum of English Departments, demanding a course of study that more adequately reflects the world in which we live. However, in most cases, that diversity has not carried over into the creative writing curriculum. Those courses continue to be dominated by a white perspective, often made visible by the lack of diversity among faculty as well as the nature of the courses being offered.

The first creative writing classes I taught were fairly traditional, with students remaining quiet as their work was discussed. I used standard anthologies of poetry and fiction to discuss and to use as inspiration for writing. My growing frustration with teaching creative writing came from the sense that students were often writing in a vacuum. Despite the reading selections they were given, the class felt like one workshop after the next with students remaining in the same place throughout the semester. My literature classes appeared to offer my students greater growth. While teaching classes that focused on diverse literature, I could see how reading and analyzing these texts expanded the students' knowledge not only of how to critique a work of literature but also how to understand the world and the various ways people experienced their lives. In these courses, I offered students the option of doing a creative project along with a critical Artist's Statement at the end of each semester. It was here that I could observe the influence of reading and thinking that had taken place for them. Transferring their learning to a creative project, such as visual art, creative writing, film, and so on, and critically discussing how it reflected on the course material produced some profoundly strong work.

Throughout the years I have taught at Hollins, our student body has become more diverse and the needs of students have changed. It was out of a desire to meet the needs of my students as well as the lack in my own education that motivated me to design the course, Writing Out of the Multicultural Experience. I wanted to create a place where the concerns of writers of color could be centered within the classroom. It is perhaps the course I wish had been available to me as a young writer. This course opens a space for students to find their own voices. As Zeyn Joukhadar, says, "Through my own processes of discovery, I am finally writing myself into existence in the fullness of my identities and watching others do the same" ("Love Letters to Those Who Came Before Me"). This course allows for this kind of writing to happen. It is time for us to interrogate our classrooms and to make sure that we create spaces where students can express their experiences, ask their questions, and speak from their identities.

The Course

I designed Writing Out of the Multicultural Experience as a hybrid course, recognizing that the study of literature must intersect with the process of writing. The course offers students the opportunity to engage with diverse literature and to use that literature to inspire their own work. My goal was to create a course that centered on multicultural writing and invited a broad range of students who were interested in writing out of various experiences. While the course readings focused on writers of color, the hope was to attract students interested in writing from different backgrounds: ethnic, cultural, racial, national, regional, and international identity as well as gender identity, sexual preference, class position, and disability. The course offered a space to push the normative white experience to the periphery and focus on identities and experiences often perceived as existing outside the center of our society.

Over the years that I have taught this course, students from various backgrounds have taken it. The course invites students with multiple identities to enter into the space and explore their experiences. Given the geographical location of Hollins University, I have had several students from Appalachia who explored their regional identity through the course. The prompts are open in a way that invites students to bring their own interests onto the page and maintain ownership of their writing.

The first time I taught the course, a student with a hearing disability enrolled in it. Her perspective brought something new to the class, and she challenged us to heighten our awareness of disability issues. She also shared an article that the students read and discussed. Inviting students to bring readings that are relevant to their experiences and asking the entire class to engage with them can be an effective way to widen the perspective of the course and respond to student interests.

This course has worked successfully for students who wanted to interrogate their various identities and their position within society. Many of them have written about their immigrant and national identities from places such as Poland, Russia, the Philippines, Cuba, El Salvador, France, China, Vietnam, Pakistan, and India. Others have explored issues related to ethnic identity, regional affiliation, biracial identity, adoption experience, class position, gender identity, sexual preference, mental illness, and travel experiences. Several students have interrogated the intersection of identities, for example, national and racial affiliation, culture and family history, politics and national identity, cultural and sexual identity, race and class position, and cultural identity and language. Creating a course description that invites students from different backgrounds can bring together a strong and diverse group of students who can learn from one another.

While this course came out of my teaching experience in the U.S., it can also be useful to those teaching in other countries that have diverse populations, such as Canada, Australia, and the U.K. The material here invites an interrogation of the dominant framework of a society and how it affects those who exist outside of it. In this way, the course can be easily adapted to other settings, perhaps with multicultural readings that have emerged from that location.

Over the years, several international students have taken this class with me, and it has worked well for them. At times, their writing focused on their experiences in the U.S. At other times, they wrote about their home country, exploring the intersection of politics, culture, and individual identity. One student from a small town in France wrote about the experience of being gay in her conservative community. A student whose family had migrated from Chile to Argentina wrote about the political issues that impacted her. Another student wrote about the experience of growing up in Russia with an Arab father.

The course takes shape based on the students who enroll in it. Keeping them at the center allows for the focus of the course to emerge from the students. Each time the class is taught, students guide the discussion and their writing creates the content of the course.

The Book

This book offers guidance to instructors, especially in the first sections. Creating the Classroom includes information about Class Size, Class Level, Confidentiality, Workshop Style, Reading Work Aloud, Literature Discussion, Literary Papers, and Creative Prompts. Writing, Reading, and Responding discusses different ways to set up writing assignments, including In-class Writing Prompts, Out of Class Writing and Reading in Class, and Out of Class Writing and Responding. The Portfolios' section discusses how the final portfolio can be designed to guide students toward becoming good editors of their work through Revisions, Revision Notes, and the Reflection Statement.

The second part of the book is addressed primarily to students. After a discussion of the importance of establishing a writing ritual, the book moves to the Readings and Prompts, guiding students through the various prompts and accompanying readings. These readings are chosen to shift the power structure that normally exists in the classroom. As Felicia Rose Chavez tells us in her book, *The Anti-Racist Writing Workshop*:

I speak of an institution of dominance and control upheld by supposedly venerable workshop leaders (primarily white), majority white workshop participants, and canonical white authors memorialized in hefty anthologies, the required texts of study. And when I speak of dominance and control, I'm really talking about silence … a profound, ubiquitous silence: the nearly complete omission of writers of color in person and in print. It is as though we do not exist. (3)

It is for this reason that the majority of the suggested readings in this book are by writers of color. The readings and prompts highlight the concerns of multicultural writers. For each prompt, there is an explanation of the prompt followed by ideas about the importance of the suggested texts and how they can initiate class discussion and inspire students' writing. The recommended readings include fiction, poetry, creative nonfiction, young adult literature, picture books, graphic novels, and film. In this way, students are introduced to various genres and mediums, so that they can see the different ways authors have approached these topics in their work. Each suggested text offers an alternative approach to writing, opening the door for students to experiment with different genres in their own work. Some texts are referenced several times for multiple prompts, allowing students to use a single work for various options in their writing. Following the prompts is a section that includes ideas for different approaches and suggestions for experimentation related to multicultural writing.

The next section brings in the voices of other multicultural writers and teachers. Each author shares their experiences on writing and teaching from their perspective. This allows the readers of this book to learn from these writers and teachers and also to see themselves within a larger multicultural community.

This book is based on my many years of teaching experience. It draws on the knowledge I have gained from teaching both creative writing and literature. The approach is one that views the study of literature and the art of creative writing as being inevitably interlinked. My education, my teaching, and my writing over the years have always presented the study of literature and the practice of creative writing as a pattern that weaves together, where neither can exist without the other. In this way, students come to see their work as participating in the larger community of writers. Their work responds to and is inspired by the reading process.

Throughout the book, I draw on what I have learned during my years of teaching, moving through the daily act of teaching a class that is meaningful for all students. At the heart of this textbook is the vision of creating a classroom where students can be all of who they are, where they don't have to leave out any part of themselves, where we understand that when we read and when we write, we bring all of ourselves to the task.

How to Use This Book

This book can be used by instructors and/or students. Instructors can use the book to design a course and have students read it to guide their writing through selected prompts. Students can use the book on their own to create a plan for developing their writing by making their way through selected readings and prompts. They can find the focus that appeals most to them and identify those readings and prompts that speak to their experiences as they pursue the subjects they wish to explore in their writing.

Several types of classes can be designed based on this book. A class such as the one I have been teaching focused on writing from the multicultural experience is one option. It is also possible to adapt the class to a particular genre, such as fiction, poetry, or creative nonfiction, selecting relevant readings and bringing in discussion related to how multicultural writers have expanded and manipulated those genres. Another one of my hybrid courses is Reading and Writing Memoir, which uses aspects of this book.

Another way to design a course using this material is to focus on a particular theme. For example, it is possible to select readings and prompts that explore the immigrant experience and then invite students to write out of their own immigrant experience. This does not need to apply to only first or second-generation immigrants, since in some way, all of us have a history of immigration that can be investigated. The course can also be adapted to focus on a more international perspective. By selecting those texts that emerge from other cultures, the course can offer a wider perspective on global literature.

While this book invites a hybrid approach, combining literature and creative writing, the balance between the two can be set up by the instructor. There can be more emphasis on analyzing literature and writing critical papers with only a few creative assignments or there can be fewer critical papers and more creative work.

The courses designed from this book can be taught by an instructor from any background. It requires a willingness to center the needs of multicultural students and to provide a space for them to bring their concerns into the classroom. The instructor needs to reconsider their position within the class and to reimagine the classroom as a place where students who have been marginalized can be at the center of the discussion.

For Teachers: Designing the Course

The following section is intended for teachers to guide them in setting up this course. The information can be used when planning assignments, discussions, and workshops. This is the foundation on which the class is built. The goal is to give students greater autonomy in the classroom and the opportunity to establish and pursue their own goals as writers. The following ideas are an invitation to think in new and more inclusive ways about how to design a course that places issues relevant to multicultural students at the center.

Creating the Classroom

Class Size

My Writing Out of the Multicultural Experience course is capped at twelve students. Eight to twelve is perhaps the ideal size for this course, because it is important to establish a close community, which is easier with fewer students. However, such small classes are not possible at many universities. If the class is larger, it would be helpful to occasionally divide into smaller groups. The readings can be discussed in separate groups and then each group can present the material to everyone. It is important to hold the first workshops with the entire class in order to establish the format. After that, students could be divided into smaller workshop groups.

Class Level

The material in this book can be used to design a course at any level from high school to graduate classes, choosing the appropriate readings and writing prompts for the students.

At the undergraduate level, the course works best if students have completed one year of college. It can also work well at the graduate level in an MFA, MA, or PhD program. I teach this course as an upper-level literature/creative writing class with the only prerequisite being junior standing. One advantage of this is that students outside of the English major often gravitate toward the class. I have had students from various disciplines, including Business, Film, Spanish, Psychology, Art History, Gender and Women's Studies, and Sociology. My course is cross-listed at the graduate level, and it has attracted students in our Creative Writing MFA program as well as our Language Teaching Assistants who come from Spanish and French speaking countries and have already completed their MA degrees. Having students from such various disciplines brings a variety of perspectives into the classroom and enriches the discussions.

Confidentiality

Trust is essential in this type of class. It is important that students feel comfortable enough to write honestly about their experiences. One rule I have implemented is that submitted work cannot be shared with anyone outside of class except with the writer's permission. By ensuring that the work is limited to the class participants, students are likely to feel more comfortable writing about a variety of topics.

Workshop Style

The typical creative writing workshop requires that the writer remain silent while their work is being discussed by others in the class. In her book, Chavez explains that during workshop, students "air their opinions amongst themselves … while the writer takes notes. Per the pedagogical rite of passage, the writer is forbidden to speak. This silencing, particularly of writers of color, is especially destructive in institutions that routinely disregard the lived experience of people who are not white" (2). I began to break away from this method of the writer remaining silent many years ago, first in my advanced courses and eventually in all my writing courses. I re-envisioned the workshop as a conversation with the writer. There is nothing more frustrating than being forced into silence as others discuss your work. The discussion might focus on something the writer has already decided to change, something they are not interested in changing, something that was actually a typo, and the things that are of most concern to the writer are never discussed.

Opening a space for the writer to participate in the conversation about their work shifts the dynamics of the workshop. The writer retains ownership of their work and can direct the conversation to their concerns. They can ask the group questions, share the options they considered as they were writing, and request suggestions. Similarly, participants can ask the writer questions about their intention, and such questions can motivate the writer to better articulate their goals. In many workshops, feedback tends to focus on how others think the writer should change their piece based on their own aesthetics—this takes control and ownership away from the writer, which is especially dangerous for writers of color who have to work harder to retain that control. By having the writer set the parameters of the discussion, the feedback can shift to the writer's goals for their piece, and others can join in a discussion on how to help the writer achieve those goals. This method also removes the instructor from being the one who establishes the direction of the workshop. The instructor must also respond to the writer's guidance. In this way, students and teachers collaborate together to create the workshop. We learn the most when we are given the opportunity to talk about our writing. Re-centering the workshop in this manner allows the writer and their piece to become the focus of the discussion.

Having grown accustomed to being silent, students do not always find it easy to talk about their own work. Offering some guidelines can be helpful. The writer can be invited to talk about the following:

> Their goals for the piece
> What went well in the writing process
> The challenges they faced in writing
> The things about which they would like feedback

This can serve as a good starting point, and it focuses not only on the final outcome of writing but also on the writing process itself. At the end of the discussion, the writer might be asked to share their ideas about how they will proceed with the revision of the piece.

This workshop format is essential when addressing multicultural issues. As minorities, we often find ourselves relegated to silence. Our stories are misunderstood, and there can be negative consequences to speaking up. Voice is a powerful tool, and too often it has been stripped from us. Chavez explains, "Our lives are an exercise in repression—the everyday denial of voice—so as to safeguard our bodies. By not speaking out, we reassure white people that we are inoffensive, nondisruptive. ... Our welfare depends on a cultural imperative of silence" (23). In a course focusing on multicultural writing, it is vital to center the voice of the writer.

Reading Work Aloud

An important aspect of a multicultural workshop is to have students read their work aloud. It is an excellent method of proofreading, a good way to improve language as it is easier to detect repetition and awkward sentences, and also helpful in finding the music and rhythm of the piece in order to enhance it. When we read our work aloud, the meaning comes to life, and we can hear where the piece is working and also where it is not working. Through our voice, we create a relationship with the work. It is equally important for other students to hear the work read aloud by the writer. As Chavez puts it, "We're forced to hear the words as shaped by their mouths, by their cadence" (105).

Literature Discussion

The literature component of this course is intended to introduce students to various work by multicultural authors. Students are encouraged to engage with the work as writers and critics. Readings include a variety of genres, and there are different ways to select and organize the reading material. The suggestions that follow offer a guideline, but each instructor can create the reading list that best suits the interests of their students.

Discussion of the literature weaves together several threads of the reading process: critical analysis, attention to author's choices, and personal response. A critical approach focused on close textual analysis helps students to interpret the work and interrogate each text. Giving attention to the author's choices allows students to consider how a work is put together and the impact of those choices. This is somewhat of a shift from the analytical approach. For example, instead of asking how the first paragraph of a novel sets up the themes, the question would be why the author chose to begin the novel in this way, what do they want to highlight, and how are they creating our entrance into the story. Similarly, instead of analyzing a character's actions and motivations, the question might focus on how the author wants to portray this character and how they want to direct our understanding of them. It is a slight shift that encourages students to heighten their awareness of how authors make choices as they write and the possible intentions behind those choices.

Personal responses are often left out of the literature classroom. This class re-opens that space. Such discussions might begin with how readers relate to a character or like/dislike something in a work and then move to a deeper exploration of how a reader engages with the literary text. How do the ideas, themes, and characters resonate with the reader and their life experiences? This begins to move us toward the genre of creative criticism discussed by J. C. Hallman. He describes it as "work that reads the self as closely as it reads the examined text and that is every bit as creative as it is critical … a kind of personal literary analysis, criticism that contemplates rather than argues" (8). Such an approach allows for the overlap of writer and critic rather than the demarcation created within the academy between scholarship and creativity. Creative criticism offers a space for simultaneously responding in a personal and critical manner. To introduce students to this method of writing about literature, it is helpful to have them read the Introduction to the first volume of *The Story About the Story* edited by J. C. Hallman and samples from this two-volume anthology.

The readings also invite students to share related personal experiences. This begins the process of interrogating their own lives and aspects of their identity. For example, when discussing essays about language, students might share experiences they have had transitioning from a native language to English or learning a new language. When discussing essays about food, students can talk about the food they have eaten throughout their lives as a way of exploring how food relates to identity. These discussions lead the way to their creative projects.

Literary Papers

Since this is a hybrid course, I generally require students to write three short papers that discuss a work of literature. Students are given a choice of writing an analytical paper, a paper focusing on the writer's choices, or a creative criticism paper. These options emerge from our discussions and give students the opportunity to develop an understanding of a literary work from different perspectives, broadening the lens through which we normally approach literature.

Creative Prompts

In a hybrid class, literature and writing work in tandem, intersecting, influencing, and inspiring each other. Therefore, writing prompts should help students make the connection between their reading and writing. I have designed the prompts so they are open to interpretation and can move the writer in various directions that emerge from the readings. When I give students a prompt, I explain that it is intended to open a possibility. The prompts nudge students to try new things—a different subject, a different approach—to take more risks with their writing. If the prompt begins to feel restrictive, they are free to manipulate it or even deviate from it. In this way, students maintain ownership of their writing and find a way to use the prompt to suite their interests. The work they submit will be considered on its own merit, not judged by how well they followed the prompt. This situates the act of writing in the writer's hands. The prompt is a possibility rather than a prescription.

In this course, students are invited to write in the genre of their choice. They may respond to the prompt with a poem, an essay, a story, or an experimental piece. While these prompts tend to direct students toward creative nonfiction, and many students choose to pursue that option, they are free to take a leap into any genre.

Writing, Reading, and Responding

In-Class Writing Prompts

I set up the first three prompts as in-class writing. Right after we have discussed the literature, I give students the prompt and allow them ten to fifteen minutes to write in class. They should begin writing immediately and should not stop until the time is up. This forces them to relinquish those moments when they sit and think about what they are going to write. During those moments, ideas are often rejected because of fear of how others might respond to them or concern that they are not good enough. Immediate in-class writing forces students to put their first thoughts on paper, to take more risks, and to bring deeper emotions onto the page. The writing and thinking process takes place simultaneously, allowing for discovery to happen. This is especially important for writers of color who struggle with self-censorship, that constant awareness of what they're allowed to reveal on the page and how others might respond to it. With everyone writing simultaneously, there is a shared experience that puts students in an equal place.

Students are often surprised by the direction their writing takes and the material that emerges when there is no opportunity for censorship. This also allows them to see how thinking and writing are simultaneous activities. So often, we are taught to separate those processes—first we think, then we do an outline, then we write. While that may work for some people and for certain kinds of writing, it can also lead to a predictability in the ideas that emerge. It leaves little room for spontaneity, for finding connections, for making discoveries. Through in-class writing, students learn what they think through the process of writing. Some of the students' best work often occurs during these in-class exercises.

Workshopping in-class writing needs to be directed away from critique and toward development. We ask the writer what they discovered in this act of writing and what they want to continue to pursue. I encourage other students to point out what appeals to them, what is interesting, what catches their attention, and then move to how the writer might continue to develop the piece and the possible directions it could take. In this way, we move away from evaluating the work based on whether or not it is polished and ready for publication and toward an exploration of how ideas take shape and develop, "as an idea in progress" (Chavez 129).

Out of Class Writing and Reading in Class

The next three or four assignments are written outside of class. Copies are distributed, and the writer reads their entire piece aloud. The workshop discussions on these pieces encourage students to take in the work both orally and visually as they are listening and following on the page at the same time. Before inviting students to comment, it is important to give the writer a chance to introduce their piece and to explain any struggles or concerns they have experienced in the writing process. This helps to set the direction of the feedback the student receives, ensuring that it will be useful to them. One of the benefits of this method is that the writer receives the first impressions of the reader and a more honest response regarding the emotional impact of the piece. During the discussion, students offer verbal feedback and also jot down a few comments to hand back to the student.

Out of Class Writing and Responding

It is important to have some assignments where students read them at home and write more extensive comments before class discussion. There are two types of assignments for which I usually do this. One is a revision assignment that asks students to take one of their in-class writing prompts and develop it fully. This exercise is useful in several ways as it allows students to see how a short writing exercise can lead to a longer and more developed piece. There is a certain excitement within the class in seeing how the piece has grown from its original state. The other type of take-home assignment is the self-designed one that comes at the end of the course. This is an opportunity for students to draw on everything they have done in class and develop their own assignment. They might write a completely new piece, they might expand a previous assignment, or they might combine several pieces they wrote into a cohesive piece. Critiquing these assignments before class discussion allows for a closer reading of the work and more detailed feedback.

Portfolios

A key component of most creative writing classes is the final portfolio in which the student presents several revised pieces as a way to show that their writing has improved through participation in the course. Those revisions are often judged by how well the student has followed the critique offered by their classmates and especially their instructor. By setting up the portfolio in this manner, editorial power is stolen from the writer. Chavez encourages us to change this model by saying, "Let's relinquish control as workshop leaders and instead challenge participants to own their personal learning journeys" (39). This can help to move us toward a different vision of the final portfolio.

Revisions

At the end of the semester, I ask students to submit a portfolio containing revisions of some of their pieces, revision notes, and a reflection statement. I don't require them to revise all their pieces. This is an acknowledgment that some pieces remain exercises from which they learn, but there is no benefit to returning to them. For others, they may not yet be emotionally ready to take on a revision process.

Widening the possibilities for how to approach revision can be helpful. It is important to encourage students to move away from the idea that revision equals making the suggestions/corrections given by classmates and instructor. Instead, it is an opportunity to actually re-vision the work. I explain that each piece requires its own approach to revision. Some pieces need fine tuning—restructuring sentences, improving word choices, finding the best opening, re-organizing paragraphs, creating stronger imagery. Others require greater transformation—deleting the first half of the piece, beginning with the last paragraph, adding new sections or scenes, digging deeper into the emotions. And yet others demand more—taking the seed of the idea and beginning again to write a new piece. Revision requires that we put pieces aside and bring them out when we can look at them with fresh eyes. If students feel stuck, they can imagine three different scenarios for approaching revision and then try each of them. This creates wider possibilities for revising. Again, it is important to emphasize that revision includes reading pieces aloud to hear our own voices in the writing and determine how well the piece is working.

Revision Notes

Students are asked to submit revision notes for each piece in their portfolio. In these notes, students reflect on and share the process they went through to revise the piece. I ask them to indicate what changes they made based on class feedback and why and what changes they did not make from the class feedback and why, as well as other changes they made and why. The WHY is crucial here—it removes the focus from whether or not they did what was suggested to how they believe the changes or lack of changes enhance the piece. It also removes the imperative that they follow the advice given to them. I make it clear that they are not obligated to follow through with suggestions given by their classmates or by me. I encourage them to think about the feedback they received and use only what is helpful in achieving their vision for the piece. The emphasis is on learning to become their own best editor. These revisions notes can be written in paragraph form, in bullet points, or as footnotes marking where changes were made or not made. I emphasize that what I am looking for in the Portfolio is evidence of a thoughtful revision process.

Reflection Statement

This statement is an opportunity for students to reflect on their work throughout the semester, their successes, their discoveries, their awareness of their process, and the direction in which they're moving. It is a moment when they can talk about themselves as writers and consider where they are and what matters to them. This type of self-reflection allows for owning the process of their growth as writers. For more information about this statement, see Reflection: A Writer's Identity later in the book.

For Students and Teachers: Readings and Prompts

The following section of the book can be used by teachers to create assignments for the course. There are multiple prompts and readings, which teachers can organize in the way that best suits their class and students.

This section can also be used by students to set up their own writing practice. It is possible to go through the prompts and readings in the order in which they are presented, and it is also possible to select the ones that are most interesting to the writer. The prompts and the readings are linked together, inviting a process that connects the experience of reading and writing. In a sense, writers can use this part of the book to create their own course.

Time and Place and Ritual

Many writing books talk about the importance of writers establishing time and place for their writing. Two of the best pieces written about this are Judith Ortiz Cofer's "5:00 AM: Writing as Ritual" and "The Woman Who Slept with One Eye Open." I read the first essay, which appears in *The Latin Deli*, the summer before I entered my last year of the PhD program at Binghamton University. Both my husband and I were in graduate school, and we had two daughters, ages three and one. I looked at my life filled with caring for my children, managing my home, and trying to work on my dissertation. And I thought, *I will never be able to write again*. My life was full to the brim, and it appeared that there was no room to add anything. It was at that moment that I stumbled into reading "5:00 AM: Writing as Ritual." For the first time, I saw myself reflected in a piece of writing. While Ortiz Cofer's life differed from

P. Kaldas, *Writing the Multicultural Experience*,
https://doi.org/10.1007/978-3-031-06124-0_3

mine, the core essence was identical: marriage, children, and work had taken over and carving out a space for writing appeared impossible. Her decision to wake at 5:00 am and dedicate two hours to her writing each morning opened a door for me. As she says at the end of the essay, "taking the time to create, stealing it from yourself if it's the only way" (168).

I had been considering making a switch from a critical to a creative dissertation, but I feared that I would not be able to dedicate myself to a life of writing. That summer, I woke at 5:30 a.m. each morning and sat down to write with no agenda, no inspiration, only the sense of urgency that if I did not do this, I would lose something that would create a hollow space in my life. Some days, I had an hour or two before the rest of the family woke; some days, I had only fifteen minutes before the cry of one of my daughters interrupted me. I accepted whatever time I was given as a gift. I began each morning still in the arms of sleep as I drank my coffee, blabbering on the page, often literally, typing *blah blah* over and over again until words emerged and revealed what was deeper in my mind.

That summer, I wrote poems, essays, and stories. I learned that I could write without inspiration, that I could write in the midst of my busy life. I made the decision to switch to a creative dissertation and dedicate my energy to my creative work. I also learned that writing that early in the morning was ideal for me. That part of my brain that was organized and logical was not yet awake, and it was the more intuitive, risk-taking part of me that sat at the desk in the early hours of the morning. In a sense, the editor is still asleep, and it is the writer who is present, the one who allows language to enter the page unedited, who can weave new words together in unexpected ways. Early morning writing has continued to be a crucial part of my process throughout my career.

I also learned the value of repetition, especially by working in the same space. When we first arrived in Binghamton directly from our three years in Egypt with our infant daughter and little money, we began scouring the yard sales to furnish our apartment. I saw a school desk that was essentially a small table. It was ten dollars, and when the seller learned we were graduate students, he gave it to me for five. Each morning, I sat at that desk in the small room we had designated as our study and closed the door. And I wrote. A familiarity developed, so that when 5:30 a.m. came, my body woke and led me to that place as if pulled by invisible threads.

Once my husband and children awoke and were settled, I went out for a walk alone. Walking gave me the opportunity to have the piece I was working on revolve through my mind and begin to clarify. The next morning when I sat down, I knew where I wanted to go with the writing. This process of writing and then walking has continued to be my ideal practice. During those walks, I can untangle the problems in the writing, and the endings of stories or essays often crystallize for me.

For multicultural writers, the need for space, time, and ritual are heightened. In addition to the daily responsibilities that everyone faces, we are also saddled with the ongoing negotiation regarding our identities. Discrimination, microaggressions, and the expectation that we must justify our presence exist as additional burdens in our lives. Creating time, space, and ritual for our writing allows us to take ownership of our own creative act. In her essay, "Imposter Poet: Recovering from Graduate School," Jessica Lopez Lyman writes,

> As a Woman of Color you know that writing is not about having a room of your own or an entire day. It is about returning to the brief moments in between office hours, before class, prior to a meeting. Carving out spaces in between the moments that matter. There is so much matter—the density of people, priorities, protests. You slice chaotic spaces into small segments of solitude. Writing requires an isolation. ... The desire to come to the page. To write and write. (20)

I urge you to establish space, time, and ritual for your writing and to lay claim to it, although this may not happen easily. As Ortiz Cofer tells us in "The Woman Who Slept with One Eye Open," "It takes a fierce devotion to defend your artistic space, and eternal vigilance over it, because the needs of others will grow like vines in your little plot and claim it back for the jungle" (88). This act of creating time and space for writing is essential for multicultural writers. Chavez tells us, "Participants concede that it's ok to put themselves first, to claim a time and space that best serves them. This is the groundwork for claiming an authentic voice" (82). Claiming your time, space, and ritual are the essential foundation on which your work can grow.

Introductory Material

"Ethnicity and Craft" by Jennifer De Leon in *Poets & Writers*
The Power of a Single Story by Chimamanda Ngozi Adichie (available on YouTube)

These first readings bring up issues that are relevant to writing from a multicultural perspective. "Ethnicity and Craft" by Jennifer De Leon is an excellent article that discusses cultural explanation, characters' ethnic identity, audience, use of italics for foreign words, language, and representation. She brings up important questions that invite conversation about the concerns we face in our writing. Beginning with these issues places the experience of what it means to be a writer of color at the center of the classroom.

Chimamanda Ngozi Adichie's Ted talk, "The Danger of a Single Story," is an excellent piece for students to watch. The points she raises about how the stories we are exposed to impact us, the expectations placed on our work to be authentic, and the importance and power of our multiple stories are relevant to writers whose writing is seen as representing their community. This can lead to discussion about the expectations placed on minority writers, the pressure to represent that can come from both within our own communities as well as the larger society.

Perhaps one of the most important points of discussion from this talk is the definition of the reader. This issue is not often discussed in creative writing classrooms. Imagining our audience is an important exercise for multicultural writers. Most of us have been indoctrinated to think of our default audience as white. This image of our audience becomes internalized as a result of living in a society dominated by white culture. "While white writers have not traditionally had to imagine a reader of color, writers of color have always been cognizant that their work would be judged and interpreted by white readers" (Mura, *A Stranger's Journey* 3). Opening up other images of a reader is essential for the multicultural writer—Do we want to envision someone from our community? Do we imagine a diverse audience? Do we imagine ourselves as the audience? The image of the reader influences how we write, what we choose to include, and how we structure our stories.

Describing her own process of figuring out the audience for her work and how it impacted her style of writing, Kandace Creel Falcón in her essay, "What Would Edén Say? Reclaiming the Personal and Grounding Story in Chicana Feminist (Academic) Writing," says,

> You will remember your true audience, your abuela who completed eight grades of formal schooling in Juarez, Mexico. You will remember your true audience, your mama who graduated from high school against the odds in Washington, Kansas. You will remember your true audience, your hermana who will soon graduate with a master's degree in technical writing with an emphasis in women's studies from Kansas State University. You will remember your true audience, your 4-year-old niece, and the young girl hungry for more, who is now searching for your book in the stacks of her community library. (11–12)

Marcia Rendon, in her essay, "Creating Native American Mirrors: and Making a Living as a Writer," articulates a similar sentiment: "There is nothing more life-affirming, writer-validating than having your audience, your people, the ones who look like you, the ones who have lived a similar experience, crack up laughing, wipe a tear, from their eye, or elbow the person next to them in a 'hey, that's us' kind of way" (89). It is possible to shift our notion of audience. We can define a community or multiple communities as our primary audience.

Another assumption that we have been implicitly taught is that if a character's race is not mentioned, then it is assumed to be white. Therefore, white writers are not expected to indicate their character's race. The underlying foundation of these assumptions is that "white writers generally assent to the assumption that race is not a significant lens through which to view their characters" (Mura, *A Stranger's Journey* 39). However, writers of color know they need to identify their characters by their race if they are not white. This underscores that "for many writers of color, the lens of race is essential to understanding their characters as well as the way the writer views her characters and the larger society" (Mura, *A Stranger's Journey* 40). If the classroom is predominantly white, it can become difficult for the work of writers of color to be understood when it is told through the lens of race, a lens that white writers generally do not utilize and may view as unnecessary. Reading through the lens of race is essential, although most white readers are not equipped with how to read through that lens, often making their critiques inadequate or even damaging. As Mura explains, "for white writers to make such an evaluation, they must be aware of the ways people of color use the lens of race to understand themselves, their communities, and the society in which they live" (*A Stranger's Journey* 41). A discussion of how to write through the lens of race and how to identify the racial/ethnic identity of characters is crucial for writers of color as they pursue their writing.

Relegating the issue of race to the periphery of the classroom and keeping whiteness centered is ultimately damaging to all writers. It maintains the belief that race is not essential to the practice of writing. Of course, the reasons for this are greater than any single classroom. As David Mura says, "This ignorance regarding the lens of race or the works of writers of color does not occur by accident. It is both a result of the racial inequalities of power in our society and a cause of it. It is part of the way the system of racial inequality maintains itself" (*A Stranger's Journey* 59). Highlighting the lens of race acknowledges the systemic racism in our society and participates in the work of dismantling it.

Many issues might come up in these opening discussions. The primary purpose is to establish students' concerns. Elements from these foundational discussions naturally interweave throughout the semester. At this point, it is a good idea to give students a chance to freewrite about their relationship to writing. They might write about the reasons why they write, when they first started writing, or how they feel about their writing. Asking for volunteers to read part or all of their freewrite can serve as a starting point for putting the things that concern them at the center of the classroom.

Identity

Write About Your Name

Our names are the beginning of our identity. In many countries, there are certain traditions for naming, and names often carry within them tribal or religious affiliation. With immigration, those traditions might continue or they might change. At times, the act of immigration transforms names. As immigrants made their way through Ellis Island, officers sometimes wrote names incorrectly, and sometimes, immigrants decided to simplify their names. That history carries through to subsequent generations. For many parents, the process of naming involves creating a link to family and culture. If parents disagree on how to name their child, that tension may become a permanent part of the child's name.

In some way or another, we all negotiate how we live with our names. The U.S. offers numerous options for this. Some people choose to go by their middle name, others use a nickname, some change their names, and others go by their initials.

Prompt: Everyone has a story for their name. This prompt is an opportunity to tell that story. You might begin by asking your parents why they chose your name. You might recall a memory of your name being misunderstood or mispronounced. You can delve into how your name connects you to family, culture, and place as well as how it may have been transformed as a result of movement from one location to another.

Readings: These readings can lead to discussions about how names highlight cultural identity, what it means to choose your own name, and the way pronunciation and meaning affect names.

© The Author(s), under exclusive license to Springer Nature Switzerland AG 2022
P. Kaldas, *Writing the Multicultural Experience*,
https://doi.org/10.1007/978-3-031-06124-0_4

"Recognized Futures" in *Geographies of Light* by Lisa Suhair Majaj
"Incantations for Unsung Boys" by Zeyn Joukhadar in *Columbia Journal*
"Name: An Improvisation on Sound" in *Looking Both Ways* by Pauline Kaldas

The poem, "Recognized Futures," by Lisa Suhair Majaj delves into what it means to have a name that connects the author to two cultures: Palestinian and American. The imagery in the poem comes from both locations as the poet struggles to resolve the tension between these two identities. One name calls up her heritage from "corn fields silver/in ripening haze, green music/of crickets, summer light sloping/to dusk on the Iowa farm" while the other means "little star in the night/.../small light on a distanced horizon" (63). Majaj's struggle reflects the tensions of being a Palestinian American born to an American mother and a Palestinian father. This poem can initiate discussion about the connection between one's name and one's culture.

In his essay, "Incantations for Unsung Boys," Zeyn Joukhadar relays the story of renaming himself. The process of coming out as trans intertwines with his cultural and familial history. The essay beautifully relays the journey of reclaiming, transforming, and transliterating his middle name to make it his own. "My name is a spell I cast over me, just as my body, now, is a spell cast each time I wake up in it. ... I claim both my name and my body for myself and no one else. ... It is the only name that has ever made me feel anchored to my body. Zeyn is an Arabic name meaning *good*, meaning *beautiful*. ... choosing the name Zeyn means not only honoring my teta Zeynab who loves me, but also choosing to call myself enough." The power of choosing his own name comes to symbolize the process of claiming identity and culture. This essay can raise issues about the connection between names and cultural/familial identity as well as the connection between naming and gender.

After giving the name prompt in class, one of my students asked me about the story of my own name. Her question motivated the writing of "Name: An Improvisation on Sound." Being Egyptian and having a Western name has always been a source of conflict for me. In this essay, I go back to the naming story I have been told and to the traditional naming practices in Egyptian culture. Being given this Western name as an Egyptian child, "my destiny as a bridge between these two languages and all they carried began. This name marked my place at the periphery of the world I was born into and which became mine" (15). Our names as individuals and as a family transformed with our immigration, and, in my case, I lost one of my middle names. I pushed the essay forward to show how that history manifested itself into the naming and renaming of my own children. This essay can open up a discussion regarding different naming practices as well as how names connect us to family. It can also invite conversation for how names sometimes change as a result of immigration.

Write About Hair

Much has been written about hair. The discussion has often focused on Black hair and the way it has been perceived in our society. The veil or hijab worn by some Muslim women has also brought attention to the visibility and sexuality of hair as well as its politics. Hair marks our appearance in significant ways and often affects the perception of our cultural identities.

Hair can also highlight the mother-daughter relationship, since it is usually mothers who take care of their young daughters' hair. If the mother does not know how to care for her daughter's hair, it can exacerbate cultural differences that cause a rift in the relationship.

Prompt: This is an opportunity to consider how hair marks your identity and how it affects self-perception. Who did your hair when you were young and how did it make you feel? How do you use your hairstyle to reflect your identity? What comments have you received about your hair? Recall a specific experience related to your hair and begin there. You can also create a character and focus on their hair.

Readings: These readings can lead to discussions about how our hair defines us, how our attempt to manipulate it reflects our identity, and how hair is perceived in different cultures.

Hairs/Pelitos by Sandra Cisneros
Caucasia by Danzy Senna
"The Benefits of Hijab" by Oula Abu Hwaij in Undergraduate Journal of
    Gender and Women's Studies

Hairs/Pelitos is a picture book taken from one of the chapters in The House on Mango Street. It describes the hair of each person in Esperanza's family, highlighting the differences. Hair becomes a way of creating a distinctive personality for each character. The story also responds to the stereotype that all people of a certain ethnicity look the same. By ending the book with the comfort of Esperanza sleeping next to her parents with "the rain outside falling and Papa snoring. The snoring, the rain, and Mama's hair that smells like bread," Cisneros creates a picture of a loving and secure family, in resistance to the notion of broken minority families. This book can create discussion about how our hair can reflect our personalities and appearance.

In *Caucasia*, we see a mother-daughter struggle being impacted by racial differences with hair as the primary symbol of disconnection. This is apparent when Cole expresses frustration against her white mother's inability to style her hair. Her sister, Birdie, describes the scene: "as my mother tugged and twisted and braided, only to end up with Cole's hair looking just as messy as it had when my mother had started" (51). This frustration pushes Cole to move closer to her father's Black girlfriend who takes her to Black hairdressers who know how to style her hair. This scene can open conversation about the connection between hair and cultural belonging.

In "The Benefits of Hijab," Oula Abu Hwaij highlights the stereotypes associated with wearing the veil and dismantles them by discussing the many reasons why a woman would choose to wear one. She explains how the veil is related to class status, religious faith, and physical appearance. She also shows how the hijab has been used as a tool against colonialism and a way to gain greater freedom in education and career opportunities. "In a world in which women's bodies are always the targets of policing by patriarchal powers, hijab has proven to be a very effective way of fighting these powers" (5). In this way, Hwajj helps the reader to reconsider the value and uses of the hijab, moving away from the Western perspective that sees it only as a tool of oppression. This essay can be an opportunity to consider how the perception of hair differs among cultures.

Write About Clothes

Clothing can be an expression of our identity, our politics, and our morals, indicating how we want to be perceived. At times, our clothing is dependent on our culture, for example, the parts of our body we choose to hide/expose, the looseness/tightness of our clothes, the dressy/casual style, and the colors we select. Clothing exists within cultural values, and our choices reflect those values.

When our clothing contradicts the norm of the society in which we live, our sense of belonging comes into question. When family restricts our clothing, our attempts to enter the larger society can be inhibited.

Prompt: This is an opportunity to explore the way you have been taught to dress. Consider a time when you were not allowed to wear something you wanted, a time when you were required to wear certain clothing, a time when your clothing was criticized or praised. How have you chosen to dress yourself in the world and why?

Readings: These readings can lead to discussions about the meaning we attach to clothing, the relationship between clothes and economic class, and the way clothing affects how others perceive us.

"Introduction" by Jennifer De Leon in *Wise Latinas: Writers on Higher Education*, edited by Jennifer De Leon
Behold the Dreamers by Imbolo Mbue
"Hijab Scene #3" and "Hijab Scene #2" in *E-mails from Scheherazad* by Mohja Kahf

In her Introduction to *Wise Latinas*, Jennifer De Leon tells the story of her college graduation dress. The perfect dress that she and her mother see in Anne Taylor is beyond their price range, and De Leon's search for an affordable dress doesn't lead to any results. The essay veers from the meaning of her graduation to her mother who was unable to fulfill her own desire to attend college. De Leon explains her mother's attitude toward education: "Education, she believed, provided a set of master keys that unlocked multiple doors—career, money, travel, health, relationships, even love" (4). The dress comes to symbolize the accomplishment of that dream. After her mother's visit, De Leon finds the dress from Anne Taylor in her closet. This essay can raise issues about how clothes signify certain accomplishments.

In *Behold the Dreamers*, we see how Neni is enamored with the high-priced brand name clothing of America. For her, they come to symbolize the American image of success, and she strives to acquire them in any way possible. The first time we are introduced to her, she is shopping for "make-believe Gucci and Versace bags" (11). When her employer gives her discarded designer clothing, Neni carries the heavy load through the subway, unwilling to leave anything behind: "Walking through Penn Station and the streets of Harlem, she had needed to stop at least a dozen times to rest from the weight of the Louis Vuitton on her right shoulder, the big brown paper bag full of Liomi's clothes and toys on her left shoulder, her rolling luggage in one hand, and more clothes and toys for Liomi in the other" (138). These clothes are the weight of the American dream that Neni carries with her. This novel can invite discussion about the connection between clothing and class position.

Mohja Kahf's Hijab poems offer insight into how those who wear the veil are criticized, pitied, or made invisible. "Hijab Scene #3" begins "'Would you like to join the PTA' she asked,/tapping her clipboard with her pen./'I would,' I said, but it was no good,/she wasn't seeing me" (25). Kahf also turns the lens to view Western clothing from a critical perspective to show how it restricts women. In "Hijab Scene #2," she describes the person who tells her that her way of dressing is "restrictive" as "hobbling away in three-inch heels and panty hose" (42). These poems highlight the way clothing affects perception and the narrow cultural lens through which Muslim women have been viewed. These poems are an opportunity to talk about clothing and stereotypes.

Write About Physical Appearance

Our physical appearance carries us through the world. It contributes to how we understand ourselves and how others understand us. When we look similar to most people around us, we pay little attention to difference when thinking about our appearance. We are able to blend into our environment. No one stares at us because we look different, and we see ourselves as part of the world surrounding us. But if our appearance differs from most people, we get pushed out of that inner circle. Our appearance elicits questions about our identity, and assumptions are made about us before we can speak for ourselves.

My movement back and forth from Egypt to the U.S. is marked by this experience of blending in and standing out. There is a freedom in walking down the street unnoticed. My husband who is African American with an appearance similar to most Egyptians felt this in a profound way when we lived in Egypt. He described it as "a load lifted off my back"—being able to walk through the city streets and go into stores unnoticed and not be burdened by the stereotypes put on him as a Black man in the U.S. was an experience of liberation.

Prompt: This is an opportunity to write about how physical appearance affects our place in the world. You might write about walking down the street in different locations, you could recall comments made about your appearance, and you can consider ways in which you try to change your appearance. This is an opportunity to explore feelings of pride or dissatisfaction about your appearance. These issues can also be explored through fiction and poetry.

Readings: These readings can lead to discussions about how ideas about physical appearance differ among cultures, how our perception of ourselves is affected by others, and how history affects our appearance.

"The Story of My Body" in *The Latin Deli* by Judith Ortiz Cofer
Arab in America by Toufic El Rassi
"Yellow" by Yasmine Anderson in *African American Review*

In "The Story of My Body," Judith Ortiz Cofer describes how she experienced her body differently in Puerto Rico and the U.S.: "I was born a white girl in Puerto Rico but became a brown girl when I came to live in the U.S. My Puerto Rican relatives called me tall; at the American school, some of my rougher classmates called me Skinny Bones, and the Shrimp because I was the smallest member of my classes" (135). Her own perception of her appearance moves back and forth across these cultural borders. This essay can initiate discussion about the cultural context that determines the value of one's appearance and the way our own understanding of our appearance is impacted by the gaze of others.

Arab in America by Toufic El Rassi is a graphic memoir that begins with the narrator receiving an email from his sister, saying, "Hey man you better shave" (1). This marks one of the ways 9/11 affected Arab Americans. In response to an event unrelated to him, the narrator must change his physical appearance. His beard now marks him as suspicious and places him within the images appearing of those who committed the terrorist attacks. The theme of physical appearance continues throughout the book. While watching a video of his class production of *The Wizard of Oz*, he recognizes his difference: "Imagine my shock upon discovering that, in sharp contrast to the angelic white faces arrayed in the chorus, the dark splotch on the grainy tape was me!" (6). Later, we have a set of photos of the terrorists with the narrator's picture inserted, commenting on the way others could perceive him as one of them. The book moves further as the narrator tells us how other Arabs have responded to 9/11 by changing their appearance. One friend dyes his hair blonde and presents a more western appearance, while another decides to wear the hijab to highlight her Arab identity (75). The perception of physical appearance underlies this narrative in multiple ways. This book can invite a conversation about how we manipulate our appearances in response to external events.

The poem, "Yellow," by Yasmine Anderson begins with various images of the color yellow: "Like malted butter/Oil's golden pool/The yolk of Thomas's rose" and ends with the question of whether or not the speaker could be recognized "Like the black bloom" (55). With its striking imagery, the poem brings into question the causes of her physical appearance and how they are intertwined with the history of enslaved peoples. This poem can inspire a discussion about how physical appearance connects us to our history and may make our identity visible or invisible.

Write About Food

For multicultural writers, food often holds great significance. Certain foods can call up feelings of belonging and/or unbelonging. The ability to find familiar foods when moving or traveling affects our sense of comfort. Food is the last aspect of culture that disappears through immigrant generations. It remains with us even after language and connection to homeland are gone. And it gets passed on to the next generation in natural ways as we participate in eating together. Often, it is not until we are older and step outside of our family home that we realize the cultural significance of the foods we have eaten. Needing to explain the food you eat to others outside of your community can be a painful or celebratory experience.

Food is a craving that is both physical and metaphorical. The desire for a particular taste often mirrors the desire for the familiarity of home, family, and culture. Every time I have moved, the first thing I try to find is a Middle Eastern grocery store. Being able to acquire the foods I know and crave assures me that I will be able to make a home for myself in my new location.

Prompt: This prompt can take you in many directions—you can write about how food relates to your identity and sense of belonging, an experience of encountering unfamiliar foods, a time when you cooked for someone or someone cooked for you, having your food questioned or needing to explain it to others.

Readings: These readings can lead to discussions about the connection between food and culture, the way food is passed on through the generations, and the perception of different types of food.

> "The Latin Deli" in *The Latin Deli* by Judith Ortiz Cofer
> "In a Leaf of Collard, Green" by Jessica Harris in *We Are What We Ate: 24 Memories of Food*, edited by Mark Winegardner
> "Don't Ask, Just Eat" by Gish Jen in *We Are What We Ate: 24 Memories of Food*, edited by Mark Winegardner

The poem, "The Latin Deli," by Judith Ortiz Cofer focuses on food as a location. The grocery store with its food items and smells recalls home for those who enter it. It becomes a gravitational space that draws in people. The woman who runs the store serves as a nourishing figure who feeds the community. As the poem proceeds, it becomes clear that food is the emblem for the loss and longing that these customers carry with them: "when they walk down the narrow aisles of her store/reading the labels of packages aloud, as if/ they were the names of lost lovers" (3). This poem can generate ideas about ethnic grocers, the connection between food and home, and how food can reflect a sense of loss and sustenance.

Jessica Harris's "In a Leaf of Collard, Green" relates the story of how food is passed down generation to generation and carried across geography and time. We follow the writer on her journey as she comes to an understanding of what has been given to her and then finds ways to transform those food traditions to suit her own location and identity. The focus on her grandmother's greens becomes the thread that ties her back to her Southern culture and even further as she recognizes that "Not only were Grandma Harris's greens southern; their manner of preparation extended back over time and across an ocean" (108). She carries this with her and finds "new ways to prepare the collards and other leaves that have become one of my culinary hallmarks," (108) showing how certain foods transform while still holding an attachment to home. This essay can help us consider how we carry/don't carry our food traditions with us. It can also invite discussion about how food travels over time and place and transforms in the process.

In "Don't Ask, Just Eat," Gish Jen shows how food can create a disjointedness in one's life. The author explores the difference between how she learned to relate to food and American social attitudes. The essay highlights how what is familiar to one person can be strange to another. Jen traces her family's attitude toward food back to her parents coming from "a culture intimate with famine … a culture that defines food broadly but prepares it with surpassing finesse" (124). This essay can call up memories of having your food criticized by others or of encountering food that is unfamiliar to you.

Write About Language

Given that language is the primary tool for a writer, understanding the languages we hear and speak is essential to our writing process. Language impacts us in ways that we do not always stop to consider. The power of knowing more than one language manifests itself when we sit down to write. We can bring these multiple languages to the page, and they can speak to each other, creating not only a linguistic layering but also expressing different visions of the world. At times, writers who bring other languages into their writing have been criticized for making their work inaccessible. Such criticism misses the point of what it means to create a text that moves beyond a monolingual story. The way we speak, the way we put our words together creates meaning, and often we cannot tell our stories without intertwining our languages.

When I arrived in the U.S. at the age of eight, I did not understand the English I heard. The words collapsed into one another, and I was unable to decipher meaning. Eventually, the language untangled, and I began to understand, to speak, and most importantly to read. But we still spoke Arabic at home, and my life existed in two languages. It was many years before I understood that to write truthfully, I had to find a way to bring these two languages to the page. When I was working on the poem, "Egypt, The War of 1967" and trying to recollect my memories from when I was six years old, I heard the words spoken in Arabic. The attempt to translate those words in English did not work. When the man walking down the street said "tafoo el noor," the repetition of the *oo* sound mirrored his steady steps and the swing of his lantern. To have him say, "turn off the lights" with its monosyllabic and heavy consonant sounds could not grasp the rhythm of the Arabic phrase. Similarly, to translate my grandmother's words to "hurry up" could not capture the urgency of the Arabic word "Yala," repeated with its lingering second syllable, reverberating through the house after each utterance. As I complained about my inability to translate these words, my soon to be husband, T. J. Anderson III, said, "Just use the Arabic." In 1988, the possibility of using Arabic, a language that was unfamiliar to most people and that used a different alphabet, seemed impossible. When I was finally defeated enough by my translation attempts, I transliterated the Arabic words and put them in the poem. These Arabic words allowed another place to enter into the poem and honored the experience I was attempting to put on the page.

Prompt: This is an opportunity to consider your experience with language. Think of a moment where language came to the forefront and write about that experience as you explore the way you use language and how it impacts you. What languages do you speak? As you consider the response, keep in mind the multiple Englishes you may have spoken or experienced. Have you tried to learn another language? Have you traveled somewhere where you did not know the language? Have you been ridiculed for the way you speak? Have you tried to change the way you speak? What languages do your family members speak and how does that affect your use of language? Consider the things that cannot be easily translated from one language to another or consider a time when language caused a misunderstanding. This is also a moment to consider how you use language in your own writing and begin to experiment.

Readings: These readings can lead to discussions about different ways to speak the same language, what it means to speak with an accent, and how we can live and speak in multiple languages.

"Mother Tongue" by Amy Tan in *Touchstone Anthology of Contemporary Creative Nonfiction*, edited by Lex Williford and Michael Martone

"Displaced" by Iman Mersal in *Beyond Memory*, edited by Pauline Kaldas and Khaled Mattawa

"The American University in Cairo" in *Letters from Cairo* by Pauline Kaldas

In "Mother Tongue," Amy Tan shows how a single language can exist in multiple ways. Tan's mother's English is expressed in what might be considered incorrect grammar, yet it has its own rhythm and clarity. She says, "Her language, as I hear it, is vivid, direct, full of observation, and imagery" (516). When others make assumptions about her mother based on her English skills, it affects the way they treat her in both minor and serious ways, such as when she is unable to receive the medical care she needs in the hospital. The daughter becomes an interpreter, not of a different language but of her mother's English. Tan comes to the awareness that she speaks two Englishes: the "correct" English she learned in school and "a different sort of English that relates to family talk, the language I grew up with" (515). Her journey of moving from a sense of embarrassment about her mother's English to embracing it is what leads her to find her voice in English as a writer: "I began to write stories using all the Englishes I grew up with" (519). Tan also expands to a wider context as she addresses the way language can be a factor in how Asian Americans get pushed into math and science because of the way teachers perceive their knowledge of English. This essay offers the opportunity to consider the types of English that each of us experienced in our upbringing. It is also a chance to think about regional differences in the U.S. and the assumptions or prejudices that those differences create. It is worthwhile to look at the English language in a global context, remembering that English is spoken in many countries, including England, India, Zimbabwe, Australia, and New Zealand. In each of these places, pronunciation, grammar, and syntax differ.

Iman Mersal's essay, "Displaced," follows well from Tan's essay, focusing on what it means to speak English with an accent. There are two strains in this essay. One is Mersal's own experience as she struggles with the weight of her accent and how it affects her self-confidence. The other explores the accent as a living part of the way someone speaks. Mersal describes the accent as revealing the speaker's other language: "The accent's energy follows a different tempo proper to the mother tongue, and when the voice carries it into a foreign language, the result is an illusion of an attempt to speak two languages at the same instant" (185). Her essay exposes the accent not as a weakness but as an expression of the bilingual person existing in two languages simultaneously. This piece invites us to consider our own speech and how our English might be influenced by other languages and dialects that are part of our experience. It can also be a gateway for exploring our accents or the accents of family members to consider the way we live inside multiple languages.

In "American University in Cairo," excerpted from *Letters from Cairo*, I recall my struggle with language when I returned to Egypt to teach at the American University in Cairo. Most students at the university are Egyptian, but the style of instruction is based on the American educational system with the language of instruction being English. The piece recalls my attempt to find the right language for this space. "If I walked into an office to make a request and spoke in English, people were very polite and I could get what I needed, but there was a distance that disturbed me. Their manner of responding to me placed me as a foreigner. If I spoke in Arabic, people were very friendly and I felt included, clearly perceived as one of them. However, I also sensed a diminished respect, perhaps because I did not seem sufficiently 'westernized,' and it was difficult to get whatever I was requesting" (32–33). Here, language reflects the hierarchy of culture established by colonialism. It was only by combining the two languages that I could achieve both a sense of cultural belonging and respect within this environment: "When I spoke in this mixture of sounds and rhythms, people responded with both respect and familiarity" (33). This essay offers an opportunity to think about the spaces we inhabit from a linguistic perspective.

Place

Write About Home

The places we inhabit have a tremendous influence on us, especially the earliest homes we remember. Delving into that memory can bring up lost experiences and the first sensations we experienced with regards to taste, smell, touch, hearing, and sight. It recalls not only the physical space but also the people with whom we shared that space. Exploring those early memories is a way to excavate the first ways we experienced our sense of belonging both within a place and within a family.

For multicultural writers, the notion of home often remains elusive and something we continue to seek throughout our lives. For immigrants, there is the loss of the first home, and for children of immigrants, their parents' recollection of another home is often passed on like a phantom memory. Home is intricately tied to identity, family, and community, and after the first place we live, subsequent homes often reflect the attempt to re-create our first sense of home. At times, our ability to make a home can be obstructed by external economic and political forces. Many groups, especially Native Americans, African Americans, and Japanese Americans have been stripped of their homes and forced into oppressive environments.

Prompt: There are multiple ways to write about home—you can write about your first home, the loss of home, or an attempt to create home in a new place. You might also consider the way you carry home with you as you move from place to place. Home can also be a focus of conflict in a work of fiction.

P. Kaldas, *Writing the Multicultural Experience*,
https://doi.org/10.1007/978-3-031-06124-0_5

Readings: These readings can lead to discussions about how others have tried to control the homes of a particular group, how people have attempted to create home under hostile circumstances, and how identity and home are linked together.

> *American Indian Stories* by Zitkala-Sa
> *Desert Exile* by Yoshiko Uchida
> *Esperanza Rising* by Pam Muñoz Ryan

In *American Indian Stories*, Zitkala-Sa loses her home on the reservation and moves to a restrictive and punitively assimilative environment at the boarding school. On the reservation, she describes herself as "Loosely clad in a slip of brown buckskin, and light-footed with a pair of soft moccasins on my feet, I was as free as the wind that blew my hair, and no less spirited than a bounding deer" (8). Once Zitkala-Sa arrives at the boarding school, multiple restrictions are placed on her, from what she has to wear, what she eats, and the language she speaks. These restrictions are intended to remove her Native culture and replace it with Western habits. These restrictions are a marked contrast from the freedom she experienced on her reservation where she could run freely, play with her friends, and learn from the elders in her culture. This story can create discussion about how our home defines our ability to express ourselves.

In *Desert Exile*, Yoshiko's family loses the home they had so carefully constructed and must make a home in the inadequate and dehumanizing internment camps. Uchida describes her home with the plants that grew in their garden and the comfort of her parents' presence: "I remember my father in his gardening clothes ... and my mother standing at the back porch" (3). Descriptions continue of the food they ate, the holidays they celebrated, and the guests they welcomed into their home. All of this is lost when they are forced to move to the internment camp. This story brings up the way noncitizens, such as the Japanese, were not allowed to own property. It can initiate a conversation about issues related to segregation and the way people have been restricted to certain neighborhoods.

In *Esperanza Rising*, Esperanza loses the luxury of her home in Mexico and must transform herself, so she can create a new home in the migrant camps of California. One of the issues that comes up in this novel is the sharp shift in economics and how it affects our sense of home and identity. When Esperanza realizes that she doesn't know how to sweep, Miguel says to her, "How would you know how to sweep a floor? The only thing that you ever learned was how to give orders" (118). Esperanza must re-define her sense of home around family and release the class hierarchies she learned in Mexico to make a new home within her restrictive circumstances. This novel can open up discussion about how our identity is impacted when we move from one home to another.

Write About Departure

With the remembrance of home, comes the experience of departure. At some point, we must leave that first home, whether it is a forced or chosen departure. That break from home becomes a loss that we carry with us as we try to make new homes in different places. Leaving home means losing the first place where we learned how to move our bodies through a physical space. To leave is also to relinquish that memory of how we inhabited space: the places we slept, ate, and played. Fifty years after leaving Egypt, I can still recall the apartment where we lived, each room, the layout of the furniture, the garden with its fruit trees, and the terrace with the grapes growing. That physical space has remained with me, imprinted on my body.

Leaving home is often associated with leaving other people. If we leave our parents' home, who do we become once we step out the door? If that departure is not voluntary, how does it change things? When we left Egypt, we also left a large extended family, and we became a nuclear family. That shift is drastic, intertwining the notion of departure with the loss of family.

Prompt: This prompt asks you to return to a moment of departure. Consider that moment of separation and try to recall both the circumstances of it as well as the emotion. Think about what and whom you were leaving and its meaning for you.

Readings: Each of the texts mentioned for the home prompt can be used here. While the early experience and memory of home is crucial in each of these texts, there is also a moment of departure. This can lead to discussions about the circumstances that make someone leave, what they leave behind, and their expectations of their new home.

American Indian Stories by Zitkala-Sa
Desert Exile by Yoshiko Uchida
Esperanza Rising by Pam Muñoz Ryan

In *American Indian Stories*, when Zitkala-Sa is taken to the boarding school, we see the moment of separation between her and her mother: "When I saw the lonely figure of my mother vanish in the distance, a sense of regret settled heavily on me" (44–45). The ride on the train marks the awareness of how far she is traveling from home as she is subjected to the white gaze. The things she valued at home, such as her moccasins, are now objects of ridicule, and she and the other children are pointed at and viewed in a way that does not acknowledge their humanity. This scene can initiate discussion about the items we associate with our home and how their meaning shifts when we leave home.

In *Desert Exile*, Uchida describes how they must dispose of many of their belongings, including personal items, such as "dozens of albums of family photographs, notebooks and sketch pads full of our childish drawings, valentines and Christmas cards we had made for our parents" (59). Many of their belongings are sold for a trivial sum as people take advantage of their desperate situation. The woman who asks for the flowers from their garden becomes symbolic of such people, and the gap left behind in the garden becomes a visual symbol of the destruction of the Uchida home. They are given a number to identify their family when they are taken to the internment camp, an act that again attempts to steal their humanity. This memoir can bring up ideas about what defines our sense of home and what it means when we lose those things that reflect our identity.

In *Esperanza Rising*, the process of leaving Mexico requires that the family leave everything behind and transform their identities from wealthy Mexicans to poor laborers. Esperanza and her mother must escape undercover and go from their privileged life in Mexico to becoming farm workers in the U.S. Hiding in the wagon on the way to the train station begins that transformation for Esperanza as she can no longer have the comforts of her home life. When they enter the train in third class, she complains to her mother, "We cannot travel in this car. It … it is not clean. And the people do not look trustworthy." Her mother's response, "*Mija*, it is all we can afford," forces her into her new class position as she begins to learn the difficult lessons of her new life (67). This novel offers an opportunity to look at how we connect home to our position in society.

Write About the Loss of Place

Being a minority often carries with it the loss of belonging and a clear sense of home. Our connection to place can be somewhat abstract. It is the way our body feels in a particular location, it is the sensory experiences we associate with a particular place, and it is the way we experience time. This connection to place happens intuitively, and we carry it with us, even when we leave those places.

My memories of Egypt remain in snapshots—the look of the elaborate cakes at Groppi's Pastry store, the smell of the air when we drove through the desert, the sound of the waves at the Mediterranean Sea where we went every summer. I continue to carry this connection to place with me and the experience feels embedded into my bodily memory.

Prompt: Consider your early connections to place. Write from a memory when place enveloped you and you felt connected to your surroundings. You can also write about the loss of a particular place. This is a good prompt for thinking about setting in a work of fiction.

Readings: These readings can lead to discussions about how we continue to carry our attachment to place, our attempts to retrieve a place we have lost, and how that sense of loss stays with us.

> *The Language of Baklava* by Diana Abu Jaber
> *The Namesake* by Jhumpa Lahiri
> "Fifty Years On/Stones in an Unfinished Wall" in *Geographies of Light* by Lisa
>   Suhair Majaj

In her first memoir, *The Language of Baklava*, Diana Abu Jaber recalls the year when she and her family return to live in Jordan. At one point, they visit the desert where her father's family lives. Sitting in that landscape, being fed and surrounded by her extended family, Diana is cradled in the lap of their housekeeper who says, "This is where you belong" (67). At this moment, everything seems to be at peace and in harmony, offering Diana the possibility of stepping into this life and becoming fully embraced by it. It is perhaps an expression of the desire to return to homeland, to forget the loss and the duality of identity. But Diana recognizes that this home cannot be retrieved, and she gets up to find her mother. In this scene, we sense the loss of Jordan as her home and how Diana carries this with her throughout her life. This scene can raise issues about how the loss of place stays with us and the desire for an original home can be constant in our lives.

In one of the opening scenes of *The Namesake*, we see Ashima in the hospital giving birth. As she goes through labor, her mind shifts from where she is to her home and family and India, imagining what everyone is doing. "American seconds tick on top of her pulse point. ... She calculates the Indian time on her hands ... it is nine and a half hours ahead in Calcutta, already evening, half past eight in the kitchen of her parents' flat on Amherst street, at this very moment, a servant is pouring after-dinner tea into steaming glasses, arranging Marie biscuits on a tray" (4–5). Ashima exists in a kind of space and time limbo between these two locations. Her loss of home during labor and birth is heightened; the scene culminates with telling her husband that she cannot raise a child in this country and that she wants to go home. This scene can bring up ideas about how the loss of home can stay with us and become highlighted during critical moments of our lives.

The poem, "Fifty Years On," recalls the Palestinian villages that were destroyed during the Nabka. While focusing on her father's village, Majaj acknowledges that "history erased the names/of four hundred eighteen villages/emptied, razed" (89). She recreates the details of landscape and people who lived in these villages, while showing how "The immensity of loss/shrouds everything" (91). History, memory, and loss intertwine in the poem while simultaneously bringing to life what has been lost. This poem can offer an opportunity to think about how even when place is lost, it continues to exist in our memories and imaginations, almost like a phantom pain.

Write About Feeling Trapped

When we are subjected to stereotypes and discrimination, we often find ourselves feeling trapped. At times, that sense of entrapment can be literal or it can be metaphorical or a combination of the two. This entrapment can be a result of governmental laws as in the case of the Japanese internment camps; other times, it can be a result of unwritten laws that determine where a group of people are allowed to live. Sometimes it is more subtle, for example, when teachers assume that students from certain cultural groups are unable to academically succeed. The traps we find ourselves in may be visible or invisible, but in some way, they limit our choices regarding such things as where to live, how well we do in school, or what careers we can pursue.

It is important to learn about the rules that limited the lives of minorities in the U.S., such as the citizenship laws that prohibited people of certain nationalities from becoming citizens, the anti-miscegenation laws that prohibited marriage between people of different races, and the system that segregated schools. The process of overturning these laws was long and difficult, and even after these laws were overturned, their impact continues to remain with us today.

Prompt: Write about a time when you and/or your family felt trapped because of your identity, or place a fictional character in a time when certain laws were in effect and they became trapped. Consider how the situation affected the person and how it limited their mobility and freedom of choice.

Readings: These readings can lead to discussions about the impact of physical, political, and economic entrapments.

Island: Poetry and History of Chinese Immigrants on Angel Island, 1910–1940,
    edited by Him Mark Lai, Genny Lim, and Judy Yung
A Better Life directed by Chris Weitz
The House on Mango Street by Sandra Cisneros

Island gathers together the poems carved on the walls of Angel Island, the immigration station set up in San Francisco to process immigrants entering the country with a focus on those coming from China during the Chinese Exclusion Act. The poems written by the immigrants detained on the island express fear, anger, and disappointment at the way they are being treated. In one poem, the author says, "The Western styled buildings are lofty; but I/have not the luck to live in them./How was I to know that my dwelling/place would be a prison?" (40). These poems are combined with interviews and profiles of some of those who endured this imprisonment based on their identities due to an unjust law that clearly marked them as being unacceptable in American society. This book can raise issues about the way certain groups of people have been constrained in physical locations and the impact it has on them. For an excellent documentary about Angel Island, see *Carved in Silence*, directed by Felicia Lowe.

In the movie, *A Better Life*, we meet Carlos, an undocumented immigrant who is striving to build a life for himself and his son. When he buys a truck to start his own landscaping business, it feels like possibilities are opening up. That hope is ultimately destroyed when he is caught, and his undocumented status is discovered. That status is what traps him and keeps him from achieving a good life for himself and his son. More concrete examples of entrapment include the detention center, Luis's school, and the neighborhood where they live. This is a good movie for talking about the restrictions faced by those who live as undocumented in our country and the spaces they inhabit.

In *The House on Mango Street*, Esperanza feels trapped in her neighborhood. This feeling comes from economics, ethnicity, and gender. The image of a woman sitting by the window recurs throughout the novel, highlighting that sense of enclosure. The ultimate image of being trapped comes through the story of Sally who marries when she is in eighth grade, and her husband "doesn't let her look out the window" (102). Esperanza longs to get out of Mango Street and have a house of her own. And yet, it is only when she listens to The Three Sisters who tell her, "When you leave you must remember to come back for the others" (105) that she understands how Mango Street has shaped her and will continue to be part of her life. This book can invite conversation about how class and ethnicity limit the spaces where people live.

Write About Landscape

Our relationship with our physical environment often marks our first sense of belonging to a place. Whether we live in a mountainous area, a place by the ocean, or a desert space, we learn to see ourselves in relation to that landscape. It offers a sense of familiarity and comfort. Even when we leave our first place in the world, we continue to gravitate toward the first landscape we experienced. There are those who love mountains, others who love the water, and those who prefer a flat landscape. Often, that relationship to environment is a given, something we experience more subconsciously.

For multicultural writers, the relationship to landscape can be crucial in achieving a sense of belonging. Our environment impacts how we relate to our surroundings and can push us away from the place we inhabit or bring us closer. We seek those places that give us a sense of being in harmony with our surroundings, especially when other factors push us to the periphery. The desert outside the city of Cairo and the Mediterranean Sea were my first environment and ones I took for granted. Having left them, I continue to seek them out in my life in the U.S.

Prompt: Think about your first landscape and the way you related to it. Consider the places you have lived and how their various landscapes impacted you. How do you feel in these different environments, and how do they affect your relationship to the place where you live?

Readings: These readings can lead to discussions about how landscape relates to the sense of home, how we take ownership of the land where we live, and how we are impacted by the loss of landscape.

> *Esperanza Rising* by Pam Muñoz Ryan
> *Desert Exile* by Yoshiko Uchida
> "Ishki, Mother, Upon Leaving The Choctaw Homelands, 1831" by Leanne
> Howe in *Famine Pots: The Choctaw-Irish Gift Exchange, 1847–Present*,
> edited by Leanne Howe and Padraig Kirwan

In one of the opening scenes of *Esperanza Rising*, Esperanza's father is teaching her to listen to the land: "And then she felt it. Softly at first. A gentle thumping. Then stronger. A resounding thud, thud, thud against her body. … She pressed to the ground, until her body was breathing with the earth's" (2–3). Esperanza loses this deep connection when she must leave Mexico. Her connection to her new environment is precarious at best as she struggles to adjust to her position and to doing manual labor to care for her mother who becomes ill. It is once she has made the transformation to her new life that she is able to hear the land in California. This novel can invite discussion about how we can not only adapt to a new landscape but take ownership of it and make it our own.

In *Desert Exile*, Uchida describes the inhospitable landscape of the internment camps. In the Topaz camp, the dust storms are difficult to maneuver: The wind "swept around us in great thrusting gusts, flinging swirling masses of sand in the air and engulfing us in a thick cloud that eclipsed the barracks only ten feet away" (112). The soil is also hard to cultivate, and the internees are unable to grow the flowers and vegetables that were possible in their first camp. Their persistence in attempting to grow their gardens becomes a reflection of their determination to survive in this landscape. This memoir can enable us to explore the way we claim our space and relate to the land to create a sense of belonging.

In Leanne Howe's poem, "Ishki, Mother, Upon Leaving The Choctaw Homelands, 1831," the first five lines begin with the refrain "Right here," laying claim to the importance of a specific place. What the poet recounts shows this as a place of nurturing and growth that is tied both to the land, "we grew three sisters into Corn, Beans, and Squash," and to the body, "where I once suckled babies into Red people" (107). This cycle of nurturing and abundance is disrupted when the Choctaw homelands are stolen from them. The loss of this land enters the physical body: "Right here there's a hole of sorrow in the center of my chest" (107). The landscape and the physical body are portrayed as having a deep connection where the loss of the land harms the body. This poem can invite discussion about Indigenous people's relationship to the land.

Write About an Airport

Airports mark those moments of transition. While we are in transit, our identities and our lives feel suspended. We are in motion from one place to another and often that means from one identity to another. For those of us who are bound to place in complex ways, being in an airport can feel liberating. International airports in particular allow us to be among people from many different places simultaneously. Another way to look at it is that we are everywhere at once. Airports can also be places of anxiety, especially with the additional security and random selection that takes place. Depending on our identity, we might find that we are frequently selected for additional searching or questioning. This is a common occurrence for many minorities.

My first memory of an airport is when we left Egypt when I was eight years old. While I didn't fully understand what was happening, I knew that it was significant. Our entire family had come to the airport to wish us well, and I was gathered into each person's arms for that farewell. This marked airports as a place of loss for me. But now when I am in an airport, I feel that sense of freedom of being nowhere, of not having to claim an identity, of that simultaneity of being nowhere and everywhere.

Prompt: This prompt can be stretched to train stations, bus stations, or other places where you have experienced the movement from place to place. You can focus on a particular experience of being in one of these places or you can explore your overall feelings about being in them. What memories come up for you when you are in an airport? Do you feel free, constrained, or both when you are there? How have these places of transition marked your movements in the world? You can also place a character in one of these settings.

Readings: These readings can lead to discussions about how airports connect us to our memories, how they serve as a place where identity is heightened or diminished, and how they mark certain life transitions.

> "The Lebanon-Detroit Express" by Alia Yunis in *Dinarzad's Children*, edited by
> Pauline Kaldas and Khaled Mattawa
> *Arab in America* by Toufic El Rassi
> "Airport" in *The Time between Places* by Pauline Kaldas

"The Lebanon-Detroit Express," published as a short story in *Dinarzad's Children* and then included as part of Alia Yunis's novel, *The Night Counter*, focuses on an older man who takes the bus every Wednesday and Friday. He recalls his life in Lebanon, his move to America, his current relationship with his children and ex-wife as the bus makes its way to the airport. It is not until he is at the airport that we realize he is there to watch the arrival of those coming from Lebanon: "The sounds of his childhood dinners would be in their hyperbolic greetings, and the scent of his mother's evening gatherings would be in the heavy perfume of the overly made-up grandmothers and in the sweat of the young men" (378). This ritual with its nostalgia and longing allows him to come closer to the homeland he has left behind and shows the airport as a place of connection, where this man can attempt to retrieve the loss of his life. This story can initiate discussion about how airports call up memories of home and the loss of home.

In the final scene of *Arab in America*, Toufic El Rassi decides to visit Lebanon. After the political and personal struggles documented in the book in response to the events of 9/11, El Rassi still feels like an outsider. That outsider status is highlighted in the airport, especially given the way Arabs have been treated in airports since 9/11. In one frame, he says, "I decided to play it safe at the airport." The picture below the words shows him in the airport, wearing a t-shirt with the words: "Viva Mexico" on it (116). In this way, he camouflages his Arab identity while in a potentially hostile space. This scene raises issues about how politics affect our experiences in airports where our identity can be called into question.

My story, "Airport," follows two people who are about to meet for the first time in the airport and will be married. After being in the U.S. for several years, Samir contacts his brother in Egypt to find a wife for him, and his brother arranges for him to marry Huda. The story switches back and forth from Samir's perspective to Huda's as each of them considers their motivations for agreeing to the marriage and their apprehension about it. Their thoughts mirror one another as Samir thinks, "Would she be on the plane? ... almost two years of filling out forms. ... He sometimes forgot the purpose behind all this, that it would eventually lead to marrying someone whom he didn't know," and Huda thinking, "Would he be there? What was she doing going to another country to marry a man she didn't even know?" (103–104). The anticipation of both characters remains suspended in the airport as the story concludes without the reader witnessing their meeting. This story can generate a conversation about how airports can be a place of transformation in one's life.

Perception

Write About Being Misperceived

How we are perceived is at the core of the multicultural experience. When those perceptions are inaccurate, demeaning, or based on stereotypes, they impact our sense of self and our place in the world. Misperceptions can come from outside of our communities as well as from within. These issues of identity move beyond race and ethnicity. They apply to economic class, gender identity, and disability, among others. The assumptions that others place on us can be confusing especially when we are young and struggling to form a cohesive sense of identity.

What happens when you do not have the physical appearance associated with your cultural identity? How does that affect your sense of belonging? At times, we change our appearance so that we can fit into a particular group. At other times, we might purposely heighten our differences. In some way, we are responding to the perceptions of others.

Prompt: There are different ways to approach this prompt. For example, you can write about a time when you have been misperceived or a time when you have misperceived someone. This turns the lens in both directions, allowing us to explore the assumptions we make.

Readings: These readings can lead to discussions about how ethnic appearance intersects with issues of class, how stereotypes affect the way we are perceived, and how political events can affect the way we are seen.

© The Author(s), under exclusive license to Springer Nature Switzerland AG 2022
P. Kaldas, *Writing the Multicultural Experience*,
https://doi.org/10.1007/978-3-031-06124-0_6

The House on Mango Street by Sandra Cisneros
The Hookah Girl by Marguerite Dabaie
"To Live in the Borderlands Means You" in *Borderlands La Frontera* by Gloria Anzaldúa

The House on Mango Street offers a complex look at issues of ethnicity, class, and gender through an innovative narrative structure. The vignettes allow this book to function as both individual stories and a novel. The first vignette sets up the focus on economic class and the way it intersects with the minority experience. In one scene, a nun at Esperanza's school points at a house to show that Esperanza does not live far enough to allow her to eat lunch at school: "You don't live far, she says ... That one? she said, pointing to a row of ugly three-flats, the ones even the raggedy men are ashamed to go into. Yes, I nodded even though I knew that wasn't my house" (45). The nun functions as spokesperson for society's values, placing Esperanza at the bottom of the hierarchy of the social class system through her misperception. This vignette can invite discussion about how certain assumptions about class affect the way we are perceived.

In *The Hookah Girl*, a graphic book, Dabaie shows the various ways she has been perceived. Playing with the idea of paper dolls, she presents herself as a Muslim, a Revolutionary, and a Seductress. Each image comes with the stereotypical clothing and items, such the Quran for the Muslim, the machete for the Revolutionary, and a magic lamp for the Seductress (12–13). In this way, Dabaie makes us see the limitations of these stereotypes and how they dehumanize. The scene raises issues about how stereotypes affect the way others perceive us and deny our humanity.

"To Live in the Borderlands" by Gloria Anzaldúa situates the poet within her multiple identities and the space of not belonging fully in any one of them. The poem begins with the lines: "To live in the borderlands means you/ are neither *hispana india negra española/ni gabacha, eres mestiza, mulata*, half-breed/caught in the crossfire between camps/while carrying all five races on your back/not knowing which side to turn to, run from" (194). The perception of others situates the poet in a non-space where she must fight for her survival, ultimately becoming a "crossroads." This poem can invite a conversation about how those who do not belong neatly in a single category are impacted by the way others perceive them.

Write About Stereotypes

The damage that stereotypes inflict on us often has a lasting impact. Investigating those stereotypes—their source and their effect—as well as how we overcome them requires that we look deep into our culture. Being subjected to stereotypes at a young age is especially difficult since we do not yet have the mechanisms to deal with them.

Stereotypes can impact how we feel about our native culture. If we internalize the ideas presented to us by the larger society, we can begin to feel cultural shame. For example, the image of Arab women as oppressed and also sexually exotic has followed Arab American women and affected their self-perception as well as their relationships. Often, we find ourselves having to make decisions on how to respond to stereotypes—Do we correct them? Ignore them? Express our anger?

Prompt: There are multiple ways to approach this prompt. You can recall an incident where you were subjected to a stereotype or you can write about ways in which your culture is stereotyped. This is also an opportunity to explore how you have responded to stereotypes about yourself and/or your culture. You can choose to write about an experience related to stereotypes through personal experience or in fictional form.

Readings: These readings can lead to discussions about how stereotypes impact our sense of self, the sources of stereotypes, and how we choose to respond to them.

> *Everything I Never Told You* by Celeste Ng
> *Amreeka*, directed by Cherien Dabis
> "Into Such Assembly" in *Under Flag* by Myung Mi Kim

Everything I Never Told You by Celeste Ng can be read as an exploration of the way stereotypes create lasting damage not only on individuals but also on the family dynamics. In this novel, both parents carry the stereotypes that have been inflicted on them and place them on their children. The Chinese father who grew up as an outsider with no friends goes on to place expectations on his son to be popular. The result is that he is unable to be an effective father when his son is subjected to the same stereotypes. After one incident, we are told, "So part of him wanted to tell Nath that he knew: what it was like to be teased, what it was like to never fit in. The other part of him wanted to shake his son, to slap him. To shape him into something different" (92). The impact of the stereotypes the father experienced are ultimately passed on to his son. This offers an opportunity to discuss how stereotypes affect our sense of identity and the way we interact with others.

The film *Amreeka* shows how the hope of coming to America can be shattered by the stereotypes that this mother and son (Muna and Fadi) encounter when they leave Palestine for the possibility of a better life. Taking place shortly after 9/11, we see the impact on Muna and Fadi as well as on Muna's sister and her husband who have been in the U.S. for some time. When Fadi is called names by the other boys at school, he cowers, shrinking into his desk. When those same boys hurt his mother, he confronts one of them, saying that it is the boy who is the terrorist, turning the stereotype around. This movie can initiate a conversation about how to respond to stereotypes while maintaining a strong sense of identity.

Another approach to responding to stereotypes can be found in the poem, "Into Such Assembly" by Myung Mi Kim. In response to the negative questions the poet receives about her culture, she offers a memory/image/scene that presents a more accurate and positive portrayal. In response to "Do they have trees in Korea? Do the children eat out of garbage cans?" the poet declares, "We had a dalmatian/We rode the train on weekends from Seoul to So-Sah where we grew grapes/We ate on the patio surrounded by dahlias" (30). The image the poet creates is one of beauty and family, thus counteracting the stereotype embedded in the question with a more positive image of her country. This poem can help us to explore the different ways we can choose to respond to stereotypes.

Write About a Political Event That Impacted Your Life

We often view political events from a distance, but there are times when those political events enter our lives and impact us on a personal level. This depends on who we are in relation to that event. The interaction between the political and personal often creates injustice, especially when certain groups of people are vilified because they are perceived as being implicit in particular acts. Such perceptions and the actions that follow push us to the periphery of society and make us question our place within the U.S.

The impact of 9/11 on the Arab American community has been documented, revealing the number of attacks motivated by anti-Arab sentiment. Much has been written about how all Arabs have been seen as suspect due to the actions of a few people. Our nation has a history of such responses with the internment of Japanese Americans as a primary example. It is important to remember that when one white person commits a violent act, all white people are not seen as being responsible.

Prompt: Consider how a political event has impacted your life. You might research your family history and talk to older relatives to see if certain events affected them. Another approach would be to make a timeline of significant political events that have taken place in your lifetime and consider where you were during those times. The impact of a political event can be more emotional; for example, an event might bring someone to a greater political consciousness. Our awareness of our identities is often heightened or even transformed by political events that impact our community.

Readings: These readings can lead to discussions about how a political event can place certain individuals in the limelight, how it can affect an entire group of people, and how it can shake a person's sense of belonging.

Once in a Promised Land by Laila Halaby
Desert Exile by Yoshiko Uchida
"To Walk Cautiously in the World" in *Looking Both Ways* by Pauline Kaldas

Once in a Promised Land looks at how 9/11 impacts the lives of an Arab American couple in Arizona and ultimately unravels the life they have built. The cracks in their marriage and their place within the U.S. reveal themselves as their own awareness of the racism embedded in American society increases. While they are in the mall, a sales clerk calls security on the husband, justifying her actions, by saying, "He just scared me. … He just stood there and stared for a really long time, like he was high or something. And then I remembered all the stuff that's been going on" (30). The couple continue to be subjected to such suspicions from others until their lives disintegrate. This novel can create a discussion about how political events can affect people's personal lives even when they're not directly related to the event.

In *Desert Exile*, Yoshiko Uchida relays how the bombing of Pearl Harbor impacted her family along with other Japanese living in the U.S. Initially, her family continues to go about their lives, not recognizing how this event will affect them. Within a few days, their father is taken away and classified as an "enemy alien," their bank accounts are frozen, and they are subjected to harassment (49). This political event uproots "120,000 men, women, and children of Japanese ancestry" (58). The evacuation order disrupts Uchida's family as they are forced into the internment camps. This memoir can help us to consider how political events can impact a particular group and change their lives.

"To Walk Cautiously in the World" is an essay about being harassed on the day Osama Bin Laden was killed and how it shifted my sense of place within my community. The incident occurs when I'm walking to a grocery store in my neighborhood: "I approach the store and note a few young boys sitting on one of the tables outside. As I walk by, one of them yells out, 'Osama Bin Laden.' His body has turned in my direction and his voice is aimed toward me. I'm the only one walking past them. A hard rock in the pit of my stomach—fear even here in the open sidewalk where it's still daylight" (90). The essay allows us to explore the way political events affect how we are seen and how this can impact our feelings of belonging.

Write About Rejection

There are multiple ways that we experience rejection in our lives. When that rejection is based on our identity, it becomes particularly hurtful, since it is something at the core of us that is being rejected. We are pushed out of a group, an organization, or a country. That rejection places us firmly outside the circle and can lead to a sense of insecurity or inferiority that remains with us and affects our ability to enter into certain spheres.

Rejection can come from the dominant group or from our own community. At the heart of it is some unwritten criteria for what qualities are necessary to belong. It may have to do with things such as physical appearance, knowledge of language, or economic class.

Prompt: This is an opportunity to recall specific experiences of rejection. It is important to reflect on those moments, considering the cause of the rejection and the way it impacted you. How did it affect the way you perceive your identity? Did it lead you to try to change anything about yourself? You might also explore who rejected you and what they were trying to protect through that rejection.

Readings: These readings can lead to discussions about how rejection can make you want to distance yourself from your native culture, how it affects the way you feel about your community, and how it can transform your sense of identity.

The Other Half of Happy by Rebecca Balcárcel
Almost American Girl by Robin Ha
"Cairo Workbook" in *Cairo Workbook* by T.J. Anderson III

The Other Half of Happy is a young adult novel that tells the story of Quijana, whose father is Guatemalan and mother is white. Her experience of carrying these two identities leads to difficult moments of feeling pushed out, especially from the Latinx community. In one scene, a group of Latina girls sit next to her in the school cafeteria. When they realize she doesn't speak Spanish, they reject her saying, "Oh, you're one of those. You don't speak Spanish, right? A coconut" (25). This rejection adds to Quijana's sense of not fully belonging in her culture, enhancing her feelings of inadequacy about meeting her father's expectations to embrace his Guatemalan culture. This novel can invite discussion about the experience of not fully belonging in your culture and the struggle to define a sense of identity.

Almost American is a graphic memoir that tells the story of the author's move from Korea to the U.S. On the first day of school, she enters the cafeteria full of people and noise and says, "I never knew being in a crowd of people could make me feel so alone" (66). When one boy talks to her, she feels happy until he asks, "Is that shit in your sandwich?" She is unable to understand what he is saying, and he takes advantage of her lack of knowledge, making her say, "I eat shit." The cafeteria erupts in laughter, pushing her out of the community and isolating her. We see her sitting alone, with her gaze downward, attempting to not cry. The last frame positions her with her arms crossed over her body in a pose to protect herself as things are being thrown at her and the words "HA HA HA" are in large letters over the figures of anonymous students. She has been rejected by her classmates, making her an outsider in her new school. This scene can create conversation about how a community can reject someone based on ignorance and stereotypes.

The poem, "Cairo Workbook," marks the experience of the author as an African American man entering into Egypt and finding himself on precarious footing. The speaker attempts to bond with the doorman whose dark skin reminds him of home and with whom he hopes to make a cultural connection, but his attempt doesn't work: "The Nubian doorman looking like back home/brother at downtown crossing/when he went to shake his hand/there was something alien to it" (11). The speaker falters as the doorman doesn't return his feeling of familiarity and this attempt to place himself in the same cultural circle. This poem raises issues about our attempts to establish a sense of belonging and what happens when those attempts fail.

Write About Hiding Yourself

There are times when our difference makes us hyper visible, so we attempt to hide ourselves. Invisibility can be done in various ways. You might choose to sit at the back of the classroom, you might grow your hair so it covers your face, or you might work to remove your accent or change the way you dress. You might even create an alternate life story when people ask about your identity. Hiding ourselves can be viewed as an act of self-preservation. It also has immense repercussions as we can lose ourselves in the process and our ability to live fully in the world.

In middle school, I walked home with a few classmates. What I remember of those walks is that my classmates tried to correct my accent. I had trouble pronouncing my *r*s and the elongated *a*. They would pronounce things slowly and try to explain to me how to create the sound in my mouth. I complied and, in a sense, we were all complicit in that attempt to make me less visible in America, to blend in just a little more.

Prompt: Go back in memory and consider a time when you tried to make yourself less visible. What motivated that desire? Were you trying to hide a particular aspect of yourself? How did you attempt to accomplish that invisibility? What was the result? You can also explore these issues through a fictional character.

Readings: These readings can lead to discussions about why we might choose to hide ourselves, the impact this has on our sense of identity, and how we can lose ourselves in the process.

> *Homegoing* by Yaa Gyasi
> "How a Full Body Wax Helped Me Feel at Home in a New Country" by Balli Kaur
>   Jaswal in *Cosmopolitan*
> "The F Word" in *Funny in Farsi* by Firoozeh Dumas

In *Homegoing* by Yaa Gyasi, the chapter focusing on Willie highlights the Great Migration with Willie and her husband, Robert, moving to Harlem. Once they arrive, it becomes clear that Robert's lighter skin and appearance makes others perceive him as white. When they see him with Willie, he is unable to get a job. Robert recognizes how his Blackness can become invisible in this new location and its benefits. As he allows this metamorphosis to occur, he enters into the white world. "He had been to the barber, his hair cut close. He had bought new clothes. ... He didn't look like himself. ... He looked so white now, it only took a few seconds for her to lose him completely, just one white face among the many, all bustling up and down the sidewalks"

(208–209). Robert's decision to hide his Black identity makes his marriage to Willie no longer viable as he moves more into the white world, and she remains in the Black world with its borders. This chapter can create a conversation about the benefits and the cost of hiding one's identity.

In "How a Full Body Wax Helped Me Feel at Home in a New Country," Balli Kaur Jaswal relays her experience of living in Turkey with a sense of discomfort as she navigates the new culture with little knowledge of the language. It is when she seeks out a body wax that she begins to feel a sense of belonging in this new environment. Afterwards, she notes, "There was no need for introspection, apologies, or shame. This was my first time living in a country where hair removal was a fact of life for many people, and not associated with assimilation or extreme vanity." After hiding herself, this experience allows her to express who she is with greater confidence and begin integrating into her environment and interacting with others. This essay can generate a discussion about how our physical body affects the way we reveal ourselves and interact in different cultures.

In the chapter, "The F Word," in *Funny in Farsi*, the power of names is highlighted as Dumas explains how her name as well as the names of her siblings gets mutilated through mispronunciation and ridicule. In elementary school, she wants a name "that didn't come with a built-in inquisition as to when and why I had moved to America and how was it that I spoke English without an accent and was I planning on going back and what did I think of America?" (63). She changes her name to Julie and achieves the invisibility she desires, "Because I spoke English without an accent and was known as Julie, people assumed I was American" (65). Yet, this invisibility only causes her life to become more complicated, creating a sharper duality in her identity. This chapter can open up a discussion about the ways we attempt to camouflage our identity in order to achieve certain benefits.

Write About Code Switching

As minorities within the U.S., we are constantly moving between cultures. For most of us, we learn at an early age that the codes of behavior differ, and to survive, we must figure out how to transition from one culture to another. These lessons are often not articulated but intuitively learned. It may include many behaviors that we do not consciously think about—hand gestures, voice volume, acceptable greetings, our manner of sitting, and the amount of personal information we share. The ability to code switch allows us to adapt to our surroundings and to gain greater success in the larger society.

This code switching often takes an invisible toll on us, blurring our sense of identity. The authenticity of who we are begins to smudge, and we exist in duplicitous ways. When I was at the University of Michigan, I had a close friend who was an international student from Egypt. We spent time with other Egyptian students and also with American friends. He observed that my behavior changed as I entered each of these communities. "Everything about you changes," he said, "the way you speak, the way you move. You become a different person." His observation allowed me to see that I had internalized this code switching and that I intuitively adapted to each cultural context.

Prompt: This is an opportunity to think about how you act in various settings and the way you shift your behavior to adapt to a particular cultural context. Consider a time when you behaved inappropriately or a time when you were told to behave differently in order to be accepted. Consider certain compliments you might have received about how you speak or behave that highlighted your ability to code switch into the dominant society.

Readings: These readings can lead to discussions about why we code switch, how code switching involves the way we act, and what happens when code switching doesn't work.

American Indian Stories by Zitkala-Sa
Caucasia by Danzy Senna
The Namesake by Jhumpa Lahiri

In *American Indian Stories*, Zitkala-Sa is forced into code switching in order to survive at the boarding school. Eventually, she finds herself torn between these two cultures, feeling alienated from both. She works hard to earn "the white man's respect," (76) but the result is that she feels like she has been transformed from a living tree to "a cold bare pole" (97). The code switching she has learned only leads to losing herself. This book allows us to explore how the attempt to survive by code switching can affect us.

In *Caucasia*, Birdie's journey with her mother and her transformation to a white girl is an exercise into complete code switching. To survive, Birdie must forget that she is Black, creating a white identity with her physical features as well as a new family history. "Around Mona, I was usually performing, trying to impress her, but never letting her in. From the outside, it must have looked like I was changing into one of those New Hampshire girls. I talked the talk, walked the walk, swayed my hips to the sound of heavy metal, learned to wear blue eyeliner and frosted lipstick and snap my gum" (233). Her code switching is complete to the point that when she hears the slurs against Black people, she looks away. This novel raises issues about the internal consequences of code switching and the way it might cause us to lose part of ourselves.

The Namesake follows Gogol as he attempts to integrate himself into American culture. Even though he accomplishes this well, there are moments that disrupt his assimilation. While at a gathering with his white girlfriend's family, one friend of the family asks Gogol a series of questions that make assumptions about his identity. His girlfriend's mother's attempt to rescue him from the conversation only reveals her own uncertainty: "'Nick's American,' Lydia says … 'he was born here.' She turns to him, and he sees from Lydia's expression that after all these months, she herself isn't sure. 'Weren't you?'" (157). Her uncertainty about the place of his birth questions his American identity, showing the failure of his code switching. This scene can create discussion about what happens when code switching fails and we find ourselves pushed out of the dominant community.

Family

Write About Parent-Child Relationships

The parent-child relationship shapes our lives in multiple ways. When there are cultural differences between parents and children, the relationship can become a difficult and contentious one. Exploring those relationships might be challenging and painful, but it can also serve as a way to understand how our parents have impacted our lives and how they have affected our cultural negotiations.

Cultural differences can expand the distance between parents and children. This is especially the case when the parents are immigrants and the children are born or primarily raised in the U.S. The path of the parents' lives and the expectations under which they lived from childhood to adulthood differ vastly from the lives of their children. Our first sense of duality comes from the tension between our home life and the public world. If there is a wide gap between the two, those tensions are heightened, and we must find a way to move from one to the other or to create a balance.

Prompt: Think about your position within your family. How do you relate to each member? What brings you close together and what distances you from one another? There are things that you carry with you from your family—some may be a burden, and some may be an empowering force. You can also focus on a specific moment of conflict within your family and delve into the underlying cause of that conflict. These issues can also be explored through other genres.

Readings: These readings can lead to discussions about tensions in the parent-child relationship, the spiritual connection between parents and children, and what we inherit from our parents.

© The Author(s), under exclusive license to Springer Nature Switzerland AG 2022
P. Kaldas, *Writing the Multicultural Experience*,
https://doi.org/10.1007/978-3-031-06124-0_7

A Better Life directed by Chris Weitz
Madam Fate by Marcia Douglas
"Letter to Ma" by Merle Woo in *This Bridge Called My Back: Writings by Radical Women of Color*, edited by Cherríe Moraga and Gloria Anzaldúa

A Better Life is a movie that delves into the father-son relationship within the context of undocumented immigration. Luis feels the pull between his father's expectations and the outside world of his school and the neighborhood gangs. As Luis struggles with the options available to him in the U.S., his relationship with his father and an understanding of his life is what ultimately helps him to find his way. After his father has been detained for his undocumented status, we see this pull exemplified in the scene when gang members are knocking on Luis's door, and he must decide whether or not to answer. This movie can initiate discussion about how a parent-child relationship can change over time and be influenced by external circumstances.

Madam Fate by Marcia Douglas revolves around several mother-daughter relationships. The novel begins with the metaphor, "Mama said all the women on this island are connected by the laughter like beads on a string" (4). The attempt to hold those beads together creates the tension in the novel. We see several mother-daughter relationships that are in danger of being broken. When Muriel goes to the U.S. and leaves her daughter, Gracie, behind, their relationship threatens to dissolve. It is through letters and gifts that they manage to keep themselves connected, and Muriel's return to Jamaica is motivated by her daughter's pregnancy. We watch Claudia searching for her lost mother throughout the book, a bond that can't be healed until her mother remembers her own identity. The novel can allow us to explore the spiritual power of the mother-daughter relationship.

In "Letter to Ma," Merle Loo speaks directly to her mother. The letter begins with the daughter expressing her dissatisfaction of their conversations that do not reach real understanding, saying, "I believe there are chasms between us" (140). The daughter longs for the mother to understand her and the work she does as a writer, teacher, and activist. She reaches further to show how it is her mother and the life she has lived that led her to do this work, acknowledging that "there was a spiritual, emotional legacy that you passed down" (141). It is a plea for intimacy, to connect with her mother more deeply. The letter ends with referencing her own children and their awareness as Asian Americans and the position they occupy in society with strength, showing how these three generations connect with one another and how her mother serves as the beginning of their identities and strength. This piece can offer an opportunity to discuss the connections between generations and the things we learn from our parents.

Write About Parental Expectations

Parental expectations in multicultural families are often based on or justified by cultural values. At times, those expectations are related to career, marriage, and moral behavior. The tension occurs when those expectations do not match with the children's desires. Expectations can relate to the choice of a career, a spouse, or moral behavior. When children don't want to abide by those expectations, they may feel not only that they are disappointing their parents but also that they are betraying their culture. Balancing their own desires against those expectations becomes both an internal and an external struggle.

Many immigrant children find themselves under pressure to become doctors, engineers, or lawyers, professions that achieve prestige and economic success. These expectations often connect to the parents' decision to leave their country and the desire to validate that decision by seeing their children succeeds in the new world. Such expectations affect what children study in college and the careers they pursue. Resisting those expectations and making their own choices can be a difficult path. For parents, success is often measured only in economic terms while for the child it can be measured by having the ability to pursue the career they desire.

Prompt: Think about the expectations your parents have placed on you, whether they have been spoken aloud or implied in other ways. How have those expectations affected you and shaped the decisions you've made in your life? How do those expectations relate to your cultural identity? Focus on a particular expectation and consider how it was communicated to you and how it affected you.

Readings: These readings can lead to discussions about how parents try to shape their children, how cultural traditions can be used to restrict children, and how parents pass on their own unfulfilled desires to their children.

Purple Hibiscus by Chimamanda Ngozi Adichie
Like Water for Chocolate by Laura Esquivel
Everything I Never Told You by Celeste Ng

In *Purple Hibiscus*, the father exists as a complete authoritative figure in the lives of his wife and children. His daughter, Kambili, describes how the priest "referred to the pope, Papa, and Jesus—in that order. He used Papa to illustrate the gospels" (4). Her father demands such complete obedience that she internalizes his expectations of her, and it shapes her behavior in school and at home. The daily schedule he creates for her marks every minute of her day and how much time she can spend on each activity. When she deviates from his expectations, his punishment is severe to the point of abuse, thus further putting his stamp on her. It is only by being exposed to her aunt's family that she begins to recognize the control her father exerts over her. Seeing her father through the lens of his abuse is painful, but it begins the process of releasing herself from his control and finding her own path in life. This novel can raise issues about how parents manipulate and shape their children and the struggle children go through to liberate themselves from that control.

Like Water for Chocolate is a novel steeped in magical realism. The primary conflict is the mother's expectation that her youngest daughter, Tita, will remain unmarried and take care of her. This expectation is presented as a tradition that can't be broken. Her mother tells her, "You know perfectly well that being the youngest daughter means you have to take care of me until the day I die. ... For generations, not a single person in my family has ever questioned this tradition, and no daughter of mine is going to be the one to start" (10–11). The mother rules with an iron fist, controlling her daughter's life and going so far as to have the man Tita loves marry the eldest daughter. The agony of these expectations affects Tita to the point of a complete breakdown, which finally allows her to both physically and emotionally distance herself from her mother. This novel can invite a discussion about traditional expectations put on children by their parents and the way those expectations can limit them.

The novel *Everything I Never Told You* revolves around the expectations that both parents place on their children, especially Lydia. Her mother wants her to complete her own unfulfilled dream of being a doctor, and her Chinese father wants her to achieve the friends and popularity he was never able to have as an immigrant child growing up in America: "Every day, at the dinner table, ... his father quizzed Lydia about her friends, while his mother nudged Lydia about her classes" (159). Lydia's desire to please her parents and meet their expectations becomes so embedded within her that she creates a façade to show that she is fulfilling those expectations. That attempt to meet their expectations leads to a breaking point that impacts the entire family. This novel can open up conversation about how parents pass on their own life dreams to their children and the impact it has on those children.

Write About an Older Relative

Immigration brings with it the loss of generational connection. Older relatives are left behind as those who are younger emigrate. The result is that those who leave as children or are born in the U.S. are denied that connection with the older members of their family. In so many cultures, stories, family history, and skills related to cooking and healing are passed on from the older to the younger generation. But there are other ways that we learn from those older than us. As we watch them, we understand how they handle life's difficulties, how they manage the obstacles that we are beginning to encounter in our lives. They are the transmitters of surviving life's hardships.

The night before we immigrated, my extended family came to our home, and we took a number of pictures. There is one of all of us and one of just my parents and me. These pictures mark the transformation of our family that occurred as a result of emigrating, the way we became a nuclear family rather than an extended family, containing aunts, uncles, cousins, and grandparents.

Prompt: Write about an older relative who had an influence on you. Consider what you learned from them either through things they told you or from watching them. How did they influence the way you handle certain things in your life? Are there particular times when you think of them? Or write about an older relative about whom you've heard stories but you never actually knew them. Do they still play a role in your life? It is possible to take this prompt into fiction, imagining the details of someone's life.

Readings: These readings can lead to discussions about the way our elders teach us how to handle difficult life experiences, how they pass on family history, and what we learn by watching them.

Esperanza Rising by Pam Muñoz Ryan
Homegoing by Yaa Gyasi
"My Grandmother Washes Her Feet in the Sink of the Bathroom at Sears" in
    E-Mails from Scheherazad by Mohja Kahf

In *Esperanza Rising*, when Esperanza has to leave Mexico, her grandmother gives her the blanket she has started to crochet, so Esperanza can continue working on it. This blanket exists in the novel as a symbol of the lesson Esperanza's grandmother is passing on to her. "Look at the zigzag of the blanket. Mountains and Valleys. Right now you are in the bottom of the valley and your problems loom big around you. But soon, you will be at the top of the mountain again" (51). The crochet pattern is a way of letting Esperanza know that she can survive the ups and downs of life. The ability to start over is something that her grandmother experienced when her own family moved from Spain to Mexico. Now Esperanza must follow the same pattern as her grandmother when she moves from Mexico to the U.S. By giving Esperanza the blanket, her grandmother gives her the key to her survival. This novel can allow us to explore how older relatives pass on their life lessons to younger members in the family.

Homegoing traces the journey of multiple generations from slavery to the present, revealing how connections remain even when family members lose each other. In one of the later generations, Akua dreams of the woman who began her lineage and lost both her daughters: "Akua was asleep, and the fire-woman had appeared. … 'Where are your children?' she asked. … 'You must always know where your children are,' the firewoman continued, and Akua shuddered" (187). Through her dreams, Akua retrieves the past and passes it on to her granddaughter, Marjorie, who then carries that history and shares it with another lost member from her family's past. Akua becomes Marjorie's connection to the past and to her history. This novel can initiate a discussion about the way older family members pass on the history of family.

In the poem, "My Grandmother Washes Her Feet in the Sink of the Bathroom at Sears," Kahf invites us into a scene where she is situated in a "clash of civilizations brewing in the Sears bathroom" (26). Her grandmother proceeds to wash her feet, so she can do her daily Muslim prayer: "She does it with great poise, balancing/herself with one plump matronly arm/against the automated hot-air hand dryer" (26). In response, "Respectable Sears matrons shake their heads and frown," viewing the grandmother's behavior as "something foreign and unhygienic" (26). Both the grandmother and the women attempt to communicate with each other through the poet, asking her to explain their views. The grandmother asserts her right to wash her feet, recalling all the places where she has done this, adding, "'We wash our feet five times a day,'/my grandmother declares hotly in Arabic./'My feet are cleaner than their sink'" (27). The grandmother functions as a symbol of a culture that remains solid even against the influence and judgment of Western standards. Her actions hold the poet close, keeping her aware of the value of cultural and religious practice. This poem can create conversation about how older relatives connect a younger generation to their culture.

Write About the Loss of Someone Connected to Your Culture

Losing someone who connects you to your culture is a particular kind of loss. Sometimes, this occurs through death and sometimes through separation. If you are disconnected from your country by geography or if your identity combines more than a single culture, there may be people who serve as an anchor to your cultural connection. This is the person who sees you through a particular lens that helps you to feel grounded in an identity that might otherwise be precarious. When that person is gone, not only is there a loss of a loved one but also the loss of a cultural connection and the knowledge they carried with them. It now requires that you find other ways to pull together the threads of your identity and place in the world.

When we emigrated from Egypt, I lost my extended family. It took me a long time to realize that what I experienced as a result was a grief similar to when someone passes away. These relatives were gone from my daily life, and as a child I could not make sense of that loss. Those aunts, uncles, cousins, and grandparents were no longer part of my daily life. Losing them disconnected me from a family structure that told me who I am and where I belong. Maintaining a sense of Egyptian identity without them required finding other ways to create that connection.

Prompt: Think of someone who connected you to an aspect of your culture and write about the relationship you had with them and how their loss affected you. What did they share with you about their own lives or from that culture, and how did that impact your identity? How do you continue to use what they gave you as you find your place in the world?

Readings: These readings can lead to discussions about how the loss of a relative can disconnect us from our culture, how we find cultural connection after we lose the person who tied us to that culture, and how the tension around cultural connection is affected by those who hold us close to our culture.

Arabian Jazz by Diana Abu Jaber
Rise the Euphrates by Carol Edgarian
The Namesake by Jhumpa Lahiri

We often think of relatives who connect us to our native culture, but in *Arabian Jazz*, it is the loss of the American mother that shifts the balance of her Arab husband and two daughters as they struggle to find a way to live in America without her. It is Nora who taught her husband how to live in America, and it is Nora who assured her daughters that their lives were grounded in America. "Nora bent over the girls, tucking them in. 'Your home is here. Oh, you will travel, I want you to. But you always know where your home is'" (78). With her loss, they all flounder, trapped in emotional spaces that keep their lives stagnant and returning to the moment of her death. It is only by confronting her loss that each of them can release themselves from that emotional trap and begin to live fully in America. This novel can invite a conversation about how older relatives connect us to our culture and give us a sense of belonging.

In *Rise the Euphrates*, Casard holds on to her granddaughter, Seta, tightly, pulling her into her Armenian identity, although Seta continues to feel split between her American and Armenian half. Casard refers to her as "her Armenian girl" (3). When Casard dies, Seta recognizes how her Armenian identity was connected to her grandmother: "To ask, just once, how she fit all that hair into one comb? Or, when she said Girlie, did she think it in the other language? Did she think Me in the other language? Was it at night that she missed him most? Was it at night that her feet swelled with the heat of Der el Zor, the heat locked under her calloused heels?" (159). Casard's death causes Seta to flounder as she tries to hold on to her Armenian identity. This novel can raise issues about how to create a sense of cultural identity after we lose someone who connects us to our culture.

Throughout the first half of *The Namesake*, we watch Gogol as he tries to distance himself from his Indian culture. Each relationship with an American woman takes him a step further as he tries to integrate himself into their lives and further away from his parents. It is when his father dies that he returns to his Indian culture, leaving his American girlfriend and spending time with his family instead, comforted by the rituals he had tried to leave behind. "Now, sitting together at the kitchen table at six-thirty every evening … this meatless meal is the only thing that makes sense. … And only for its duration is their grief slightly abated, the enforced absence of certain foods on their plates conjuring his father's presence somehow" (180–181). The father's death marks a turning point in Gogol's growth and his ability to recognize the value of his Indian culture. This novel can open up a discussion about how children go through stages of rejecting and accepting their culture and how that connects to certain people in their lives.

Write About Forbidden Relationships

The desire to maintain the identity of a community can often be expressed by the pressure to have everyone marry from within that community. This can be an attempt to hold onto culture, racial pride, economic status, religion, or other attributes that are valued. It can be easy to maintain this adherence to community when exposure to those who are different is minimized. However, with migration, the possibility of stepping out of community in the choice of a life partner increases. Our family's expectations regarding life partners are not always spoken but are communicated in more subtle ways that we can imbibe even without our own awareness. How we navigate these forbidden relationships can be fraught with tension as we have to negotiate our own feelings about stepping outside of our community as well as the anticipated rejection of our family.

Stepping beyond cultural confines in the choice of a partner can allow for the possibility of opening up to new ideas and new ways of living in the world. At times, families are able to push beyond their own values and embrace their children's decision; at other times, they choose to remain in their beliefs and a permanent split happens within a family.

Prompt: Reflect on the relationships that are forbidden within your family. How did these restrictions get passed on to you? Do you agree/disagree with them? Consider a time when you were in a relationship that did not meet your family's approval. How did their expectations affect the way you felt about that relationship? Did you hide or reveal the relationship? In what way did it affect your connection to your family?

Readings: These readings can lead to discussions about how a relationship can cause a break within the family, how disapproval is expressed by family members, and how prejudice plays a role in a relationship.

Double Happiness directed by Mina Shum
Rise the Euphrates by Carol Edgarian
"American History" in *The Latin Deli* by Judith Ortiz Cofer

In the movie, *Double Happiness*, the daughter of Chinese immigrants living in Canada begins a relationship with a white man. She struggles as the relationship becomes more serious but keeps it hidden from her parents who she knows will disapprove. Her constant refrain is "It's complicated." When her parents discover the relationship, she attempts to break up with her boyfriend but ultimately recognizes that she cannot repress her own desires for the sake of her parents. This forbidden relationship becomes the catalyst for each family member to interrogate their personal struggles and expectations. The closeness that has bound the family breaks when the father is unwilling to change. This movie can help us to consider how a forbidden relationship can cause a family to struggle as they are pushed into change.

In *Rise the Euphrates*, Araxie's decision to marry a white man rather than someone from the close-knit Armenian community in Memorial, Connecticut, causes a break with her mother who has survived the Armenian genocide. For her mother, anyone who is not Armenian is "odar," a word used to reference the Turks who committed the atrocities. Casard's resistance to George is based on his identity. When Araxie tells her about the relationship, Casard's response makes that clear: "He's not your kind. ... No. You find yourself a good man, Araxie. And that means good Armenian" (54). Once they marry, Casard continuously reminds George of his outsider status, causing the rift between her and her daughter to widen. It is a rift that never fully heals, leaving Araxie caught between her mother and her husband. This book can generate a conversation about how stepping outside of the community impacts the relationship with the family.

In "American History," Ortiz Cofer tells the story of a young girl eagerly trying to gain the attention of a young boy who lives in the house next door to her building and attends her school. On the day when he has invited her to come over to study together, she knocks on the door only to be greeted by his mother who sends her away with "Listen. Honey. Eugene doesn't want to study with you. He is a smart boy. Doesn't need help. ... It's nothing personal. ... Run back home now" (14–15). The mother views the girl through the lens of her identity, which she demeans and positions as unacceptable. She is pushed out even before she can enter the home, as the woman marks her outsider status. The door and the front stoop become barriers that are impossible to cross. This story can enable us to explore the obstacles we encounter when trying to create a relationship that is forbidden by society.

Write About Romantic Relationships

Relationships are often seen as a means of continuing and maintaining community values. While the criteria for what makes an acceptable partner differs from one culture and one family to the next, there is always some criteria, whether it is based on religion, class, family status, race, and so on. In many cultures, the marriage of two people is viewed as the intertwining of two families, which justifies the right of family members to approve or disapprove of the union. Stepping outside of the familial and cultural expectations can cause a rift between family members. When our family's values conflict with our desires, the struggle we experience as we choose a partner and our choices can have serious consequences.

Sexual preference and gender identity also play a role here. If the family or cultural values do not make room for various sexual preferences and gender identities, the conflicts that arise can be permanently damaging. Considering who you are and how you want to live your life becomes particularly challenging when there is not a supportive community. These struggles can lead to healing or permanent breaks within families.

Prompt: Write about one of your relationships and how your family viewed it—Why did they approve or not approve of the relationship? Consider your own biases in terms of relationships. Explore your culture's attitudes toward romantic relationships—What values give rise to your family's preferences?

Readings: These readings can lead to discussions about how social values affect romantic relationships, how cultural differences impact a relationship, and how being in a different culture affects a relationship.

> *Sweet Land* directed by Ali Selim
> *Everything I Never Told You* by Celeste Ng
> "The New World" by Susan Muaddi Darraj in *Dinarzad's Children: An Anthology of Contemporary Arab American Literature*, edited by Pauline Kaldas and Khaled Mattawa

Sweet Land takes us to the Midwest just after World War I, when a woman arrives from Germany to marry a farmer in Minnesota. At a time when Germans were viewed as outsiders and labeled as dangerous foreigners, the community's distrust and refusal to accept the newcomer results in both personal and communal struggles. Inge and Olaf must negotiate their relationship within the prejudice of the town. The commitment Olaf and Inge make to one another is evident in the scene when they must harvest the wheat field on their own because the community has turned against them. This movie invites discussion about how prejudice toward certain types of marriages has changed over time.

Everything I Never Told You takes us to the 1960s with a white woman and a Chinese man getting married at a time when their marriage would have been illegal in many states. "When they had married, he and Marilyn had agreed to forget about the past. They would start a new life together, the two of them, with no looking back" (126). But it's not possible to erase the past that has shaped their identities and that influences their relationship. The struggle with their differences and its impact on their children and the family threaten to destroy them. This novel can initiate a conversation about how a romantic relationship can affect an entire family.

In the "The New World," we meet Siham, who has recently arrived to the U.S. from Jerusalem after marrying Nader who had been living in America for several years. While Nader is at work, Siham practices English and the vocabulary she learns serves as a foreshadowing for what will happen in the story: "I hide. You hide. He/she/it hides./I lie. We lie. They lie./I cry. You cry. He/she/it cries./I cry" (27). Her new marriage is a happy one until she begins to receive phone calls from a woman who wants to speak to her husband. Her discovery that her husband married this woman in order to gain permanent residence in the U.S. shifts the power dynamics of the relationship between her and her husband. She gives him the money she has earned through her embroidery and which she was saving to decorate a nursery to pay the woman. What was initially a romantic relationship has been corrupted by the past which must now be dealt with before the couple can move into their future. This story can lead to discussion about how secrets can affect a romantic relationship.

Community

Write About a Communal Cultural Experience

Every community has rituals and celebrations that bring people together to participate in a common experience. Such events bind people and create a sense of communal identity. Gatherings might focus on a holiday, a seasonal event, or a special occasion. Our position within these events depends on our relationship to that community. Do we feel a sense of belonging or do we feel like an outsider? Do we accept the communal identity or do we reject it? When these events take place in a new culture, they shift in their importance. If the community is on the outskirts of the dominant culture, the event becomes a way to maintain loyalty and place value on the community.

We often belong to multiple communities and our affinity to each one differs. My family attended a Syrian Orthodox Church when I was growing up. We were the only Egyptian family at the church, and I experienced a simultaneous sense of belonging and unbelonging. The time when I felt most connected to that community was during the haflas or parties where we ate Middle Eastern food and danced to Arab music. I leaned to dance the Dabke, a circle or spiral of people holding hands and dancing together. It was this movement with others that made me feel connected.

Prompt: Think of an event that brought community members together and in which you participated. What was the purpose of the event? Did you feel on the inside or outside of the community during the event? What elements of the event created a communal identity?

P. Kaldas, *Writing the Multicultural Experience*,
https://doi.org/10.1007/978-3-031-06124-0_8

Readings: These readings can lead to discussions about cultural practices that bring people together, the creation of communal events in a new country, and making a community as an act of resistance against a dominant culture.

> ¡A bailar!/Let's Dance! by Judith Ortiz Cofer
> The Namesake by Jhumpa Lahiri
> Antonia's Line directed by Marlene Gorris

¡A bailar!/Let's Dance! is a beautiful picture book that shows a mother and daughter going to a dance where the father is playing in a band. As they make their way to the dance, they invite everyone they come across, and several join them, making the community larger with each page. The refrain throughout the book, written in both Spanish and English, becomes a call for the community to join together. "Move, move, move/to the rhythm that makes us .../ dance, dance, dance." As a bilingual book, the story shows the value of the Spanish language as well as the culture attached to it. When we arrive at the last page, we see a picture of a large group of people who are all there to celebrate and dance, showing how the music creates a communal event. This book can help us to think about how certain events bring people together.

In The Namesake, Gogol's upbringing is marked by the many Bengali parties hosted by his parents. His mother spends days cooking, and all the Bengali families they know are invited. They gather based on their common culture and share the food that is familiar to them. This gathering has greater weight as it takes place in the U.S. where all of them live as outsiders. In the enclosed space of the house, they can be themselves, and for a few hours, they don't have to adapt to American society. Gogol feels uncomfortable and bored at these gatherings, eager to return to his more American daily life. The novel ends with another such party, described differently through Gogol's eyes: "People talk of how much they've come to love Ashima's Christmas Eve parties. ... They have come to rely on her, Gogol realizes, to collect them together" (286). By this point, Gogol has gone through multiple transformations and has understood the comfort that such an event provides. This novel can open up discussion about how communal events create a sense of cultural identity in an unfamiliar place.

The movie, Antonia's Line, takes place in a Dutch village where Antonia and her daughter return when Antonia's mother dies, and they live on the family's farm. Antonia was raised in the town but then left, so she exists as both an insider and outsider to the community. Her home becomes a space where others who are outcast from the society can enter. This is marked by the table where they eat and that lengthens throughout the film to accommodate others who need a place of comfort or escape. In this way, Antonia creates a community for all those who are not accepted by the larger society. This movie invites a conversation about how it's possible to create one's own community that provides support for a variety of people.

Write About a Neighborhood

The neighborhoods we live in shape our understanding of American culture and our sense of identity within that culture. If we live in a neighborhood where most people belong to the same culture, there can be a sense of belonging and comfort. If we live in a predominantly white neighborhood, our sense of belonging can be consistently questioned. Are we similar to our neighbors or is our difference continuously highlighted? How we navigate our immediate surroundings on a daily basis contributes to shaping our relationship to the larger society.

Ethnic neighborhoods, such as Chinatown, Little Italy, and Koreatown, have been an ongoing part of the American landscape and have been viewed in various ways. For members of a particular ethnic group, such neighborhoods become a refuge from the hardships experienced in the larger society, a place where language, food, and cultural practices are familiar and where it is possible to find housing and jobs. For the larger American society, these neighborhoods have been viewed as a threat to American culture or as an exotic space to visit.

Prompt: Write about a neighborhood where you lived. Consider your house or apartment, your neighbors, the places you went, the places you did not go, and how you felt moving through the space. Did you and your family blend into the neighborhood? How were you viewed by your neighbors? How did living in this neighborhood affect your relationship to American society?

Readings: These readings can lead to discussions about how our neighborhood relates to class position, how a neighborhood can limit our movements, and how a particular place can give us a sense of home.

The House on Mango Street by Sandra Cisneros
"American History" in *The Latin Deli* by Judith Ortiz Cofer
"One Village" by Naomi Shihab Nye in *Beyond Memory: An Anthology of Arab American Creative Nonfiction*, edited by Pauline Kaldas and Khaled Mattawa

Each of the vignettes in *The House on Mango Street* focuses on Esperanza's observations and experiences of living in her neighborhood. As she watches the lives of those around her, she notices the limitations based on economic class that keep them locked into their circumstances. Her desire for a better life is indicated by the things she does not have in her neighborhood: a home with more space, greater economic mobility, and the ability to purse her dreams: "A house all my own. With my porch and my pillow, my pretty purple petunias. My books and my stories. My two shoes waiting beside the bed" (108). It is only when she realizes how living on Mango Street has shaped her that she can imagine a future that allows her to return to her neighborhood. This book can invite discussion about the relationship between neighborhoods, and ethnicity and class position.

In several of the pieces in *The Latin Deli*, Ortiz Cofer describes El Building where everyone who lives there is Puerto Rican. Although it is a single building, it functions as a neighborhood, where everyone knows everyone else and what is happening in their lives. The music, the smells of food cooking, and the Spanish being spoken all point to this space as an ethnic neighborhood that provides both protection and a sense of belonging for its inhabitants: "At almost any hour of the day, El Building was like a monstrous jukebox, blasting out *salsas* from open windows as the residents, mostly new immigrants just up from the island, tried to drown out whatever they were currently enduring with loud music" (7). It is when someone steps outside of this building that they encounter the hostility of American society. This close reading of El Building can create conversation about the way such spaces provide community and support that protects against the difficulties faced outside of that space.

In "One Village," Naomi Shihab Nye describes returning to visit her grandmother in her West Bank Palestinian Village. Her observations of a daily communal life interrupted by the presence of Israel highlight the precarious existence of this village. Nye experiences being in the village as a return to home although she has never lived there: "Maybe this is what it means to be in your genetic home. That you will feel on fifty levels at once, the immediate level as well as the level of blood, the level of your uncles, of the weeping in the pillow at night, weddings and graves, the babies who didn't make it, level of the secret and the unseen. Maybe this is heritage, that root that gives you more than you deserve" (216). The village grounds her in family, history, and culture, giving her a foundation on which she can build her life and identity. This essay opens up ideas about how a particular neighborhood can be of significance even when we have not lived there.

Write About a School Experience

School is a place where difference and the responses to difference play out in visible ways. School is the first place where we go when we step out of the private world of our family and into the public world to enter a new community. It is the first place where we begin to notice difference in the way someone looks, speaks, and dresses or the food they eat. Children can be kind or cruel when they encounter differences. School is the first community we enter where we must figure out a way to belong. The need to create a unified and homogeneous community often dominates the school environment.

As we try to fit into our school, we might begin to make changes in our appearance, clothing, or the food we bring to lunch. This can be seen as our first attempt to mold to our various communities and our awareness that our identity can be malleable.

Prompt: Think about an experience you had in school or imagine one for a character. What is the culture of the dominant group? How do you fit in or don't fit in? How were you made to feel like an outsider and how did you respond to that? Did you attempt to change anything about yourself so that you could belong?

Readings: These readings can lead to discussions about the way differences can create greater understanding, the cultural limitations of teachers, and the racial hierarchy that exists in schools.

> *The Sandwich Swap* by Queen Rania Al Abdullah
> "Turtle Came to See Me" by Margarita Engle in *Enchanted Air*
> "Same Old Story" in *River to Cross* by T.J. Anderson III

In the picture book, *The Sandwich Swap*, by Queen Rania Al Abdullah, we meet two friends who have many things in common except that they think each other's lunches look gross. One has a peanut butter and jelly sandwich, and the other has a pita and hummus sandwich. Their conflict erupts with the kids at school taking sides and calling each other "stupid" and "weird," culminating in a food fight. When the two girls taste each other's sandwiches, they discover both are good: "Hey, this is delicious!" "And this is heavenly!" The story ends with a fold out page that reveals a large table where each student has a dish in front of them with the flag of their country. On either end of the table are the two girls who created the opportunity for everyone to taste each other's food. This story shows how the lack of understanding can erupt into a war-like situation. It also indicates that with knowledge comes understanding and cooperation, making a political statement. This book can be a good way to discuss the positive consequences of learning about each other's culture.

The poem, "Turtle Came to See Me," recalls a picture the poet drew in kindergarten of "a bright crayon picture/of a dancing tree, the branches/tossed by island wind." Her teacher reprimands her, saying, "REAL TREES/DON'T LOOK LIKE THAT." The poet must assert her own knowledge against the authority of her teacher, realizing that "that teachers/can be wrong./They have never seen/the dancing plants/of Cuba" (22). This allows the poet to place her cultural experience above the limitations of the school system. This poem can invite discussion about how school experiences attempt to create conformity and cultural hierarchy.

The poem, "Same Old Story," recalls an encounter between a young Black man and his guidance counselor. Arriving with a list of books by Black writers that he wants to read, the counselor tells him, "he best be reading the classics/ unless he want to grow up/and be a professional black" (37). Rather than a direct response, the poem moves to reference Nina Simone and Nelson Mandela, calling up the art and politics of African peoples. Ending with "I ain't going to let nobody turn me around," (37) a reference to an important protest song during the Civil Rights movement, the poem becomes a response to the ignorance of the guidance counselor and an assertion of the power and history of being Black. This poem raises issues about how minority students have been denied access to learning about their own culture and history within the school system.

Write About a Holiday

Holidays are marked by rituals, traditional practices, food, and gatherings. They instill a sense of communal identity. When we celebrate those holidays in a place where others are also celebrating them, we become part of a larger community and our practices are validated. We feel that we are connected to something larger than ourselves. However, when we exist as a minority in a country, the practice of these holidays becomes something that marks our difference. Those celebrations can pull us away from belonging in the larger culture. Whether our traditions include fasting, eating specific foods, or attending religious services, they become something we have to explain rather than something that affirms our communal identity. Additionally, if we do not celebrate the holidays celebrated by the majority, we are pushed out even further. This process can simultaneously create feelings of cultural pride and shame.

For me, something as simple as celebrating Easter at a different time because my family is Coptic Orthodox pushed me out of the center. I did not understand why we didn't celebrate with everyone else, so I could never offer a clear explanation to those who asked. The practice of Coptic fasting before Easter and Christmas, which requires a vegan diet, was equally difficult to explain, especially in the 1970s.

Prompt: Think about the holidays you celebrated as a child and the ones you celebrate now. How did they shape your sense of identity within your community? You can also take time to describe the celebration of a holiday, to bring in the details, the people, the food, and to evoke the emotions that accompany that celebration. You can also write a fictional scene that takes place during a holiday.

Readings: These readings can lead to discussions about how families balance the celebration of multiple holidays, how celebrations bind a community together, and how the traditions of a holiday can change due to immigration.

"Me and Bob Hope" in *Funny in Farsi* by Firoozeh Dumas
Rise the Euphrates by Carol Edgarian
"In the Direction of Home" by Pauline Kaldas in *Home: An Imagined Landscape*,
    edited by Marjorie Agosín

In the chapter, "Me and Bob Hope," in *Funny in Farsi*, Dumas talks about feeling left out during Christmas celebrations, saying, "To be left out of Christmas is the ultimate minority experience" (107). In Iran, the biggest holiday, celebrated by people of all religions is Nowruz (New Year's Day). It is a holiday that is prepared for and celebrated with great festivities. That excitement and sense of celebration is lost once Dumas's family comes to the U.S. The sense of communal celebration disappears. Dumas explores how these holidays affect her sense of belonging in America with humor and insight. This essay can create discussion about the experience of celebrating holidays in different locations.

In *Rise the Euphrates*, the family celebrates Christmas twice, once with the Catholic calendar and once with the Armenian Orthodox calendar. While Seta's father attempts to present this as a sign that they are twice as lucky, Seta learns that this duality marks her lack of full belonging in either community and threatens to fragment her family. This becomes apparent during one Armenian Orthodox Christmas dinner when Seta's grandmother says, "Your father must be disappointed we don't serve none of that Episcopalian Jell-O salad" (100). Her purposeful comment pushes Seta's American father outside of the Armenian circle and highlights his difference, reclaiming this holiday as a space for only those who are fully Armenian. This scene can invite discussion about how holidays create a sense of community and who is allowed into that community.

Home: An Imagined Landscape, edited by Marjorie Agosín, is an anthology that offers multiple perspectives on home by multicultural writers. When I wrote my essay, "In the Direction of Home," for this anthology, what surprised me was the number of times that I returned to describing the celebration of Christmas. "Each Christmas, we invite our American friends—this attempt to fabricate home, to create family from friendships instead of the blood that binds us. ... I am inside and outside my Christmas gathering— there are grape leaves and spinach filo along with turkey and cranberry sauce, and I am dislocated in the limbo of lost and found homes" (9–10). These scenes open up the notion of transformative identity and the sense of being in more than a single location. I had not realized the impact of my parents' celebration of the holiday after we came to the U.S. or the way that I had continued that tradition of gathering people in my American life. This essay can allow us to explore how we carry holiday traditions with us when we move from one place to another.

Write About Class Position and Cultural Identity

Intersectionality offers a way to explore our multiple identities and how we live in those identities simultaneously. Thinking in particular about cultural and class identity offers an interesting lens into our position in the world. How are we perceived when we are part of a minority and also part of the upper class? How does that change if we are part of the working class? What communities does our class position allow us to enter that we might not otherwise have access to? One's socioeconomic class holds a lot of power in our society and often shifts the way others perceive us and the communities in which we can participate.

Certain assumptions are made about the class position of minorities, often assuming that they are of a lower class or hold jobs considered more menial. When my father-in-law who is African American and a professor entered a bank, carrying an envelope with the deposit for the house he was purchasing, he was assumed to be a delivery person. When I tell someone that I am professor, I see how their perception of me shifts, how they become willing to make room for me, although always with caution.

Prompt: Think about a time when your class and cultural identity intersected and affected the community you could enter. What assumptions were being made about you? Has your class position ever kept you out of a community? Does your class and culture ever feel like they conflict with one another?

Readings: These readings can lead to discussions about the things we associate with certain class positions, the way we use our class position to protect us, and how the places we live are related to our economic status.

> *Behold the Dreamers* by Imbolo Mbue
> *Once in a Promised Land* by Laila Halaby
> "Community Interrupted" in *When They Call You a Terrorist: A Black Lives Matter Memoir* by Patrisse Khan-Cullors

In many ways, *Behold the Dreamers* is all about class. Jende comes to America from Cameroon to gain economic success so that Neni's father will allow him to marry her. In America, Jende and Neni strive to reach that success. Neni attends college to become a pharmacist, so she can have status and a high paying job. When their son, Liomi, aspires to be a chauffeur like his father, his mother quickly says, "Nobody chooses to be a chauffeur. ... A chauffeur is a good job for Papa, but it won't be for you" (68). Their minority status keeps them situated in a lower class even as they strive to step out of it. This novel can create a discussion about how certain restrictions keep minorities from succeeding economically and how wealth is often seen as a way to shed the discrimination that comes with being a minority.

In *Once in a Promised Land*, we meet Jassim and Salwa after they have been living in America for a number of years. They have achieved the elements of the American dream; both have good jobs and they live in an upper-class neighborhood. This status allows them to traverse their world with ease. Their Arab identity is subsumed within their class status. It is when 9/11 happens that their class position can no longer protect them, and their race becomes the prominent feature through which others see them and find them suspicious. When Jassim is questioned by the FBI, he attempts to exonerate himself by saying, "I am a normal citizen who happens to be as Arab" (232). Right after 9/11, one of Salwa's colleagues gives her American flag decals and says, "You should put one on your car, on the back window. You never know what people are thinking, and having this will let them know where you stand" (55). Jassim and Salwa are pushed out of the society, which they have strived to enter. This novel can raise issues regarding how class and cultural identity intersect in complex ways.

In the first chapter of her memoir, "Community Interrupted," Khan-Cullors describes the neighborhood where her family lives: "Ours is a neighborhood designed to be transient, not a place where roots are meant to take hold, meant to grow into trees that live and live. ... My own mother worked 16 hours a day, at two and sometimes three jobs. She never had a career, only labored to put together enough to make ends meet. Telemarketer, receptionist, domestic support, office cleaner—these were the jobs my mom did and all were vital to us" (11–12). Through these descriptions, we see how class is embedded into this location and the identity of those who live there. The comparison to the wealthy white neighborhood of Sherman Oaks, only a mile away, makes it clear that race and class are intricately connected. This memoir can help us to think about how our specific geographical location determines the way we see our class position.

Write About Music

The first music we hear is often one that is intimately connected to our culture. We hear it within our community, and it weaves into our sense of identity. Music speaks from an individual voice that connects those who are listening to the larger community. It creates a communal identity through history and culture as expressed through music.

In every culture, there have been certain musicians who emerged as iconic figures and transformed the culture through their music. It is interesting to consider why these figures have such a strong following and how they bring people together. What is the relationship between musician and listener? What is happening at that moment in history and how does the musician speak to it? How does that music transform the community?

Prompt: Think about a specific song that has been significant for you—consider the meaning of that song within the larger community as well as its personal meaning for you. You can also focus on a particular musician whose work has been meaningful to you. This can also be an opportunity to bring music into a work of fiction or poetry to heighten the narrative.

Readings: These readings can lead to discussion about the way a certain song affects the community, the impact of a singer on the larger culture, and the way music can create connections among people.

"billie lives! billie lives" by Hattie Gossett in *This Bridge Called My Back: Writings by Radical Women of Color*, edited by Cherríe Moraga and Gloria Anzaldúa
"Zai El-Hawa" in *Ismailia Eclipse* by Khaled Mattawa
"the hotel worker" in *t/here it is* by T.J. Anderson III

"billie lives! billie lives" by Hattie Gossett begins with the proclamation that "yeah billi holiday lives." She places Billi Holiday in a house with other jazz musicians and activists like Ma Rainey, John Coltrane, Tammi Terrel, Sojourner Truth, Fannie Lou Hammer, and Stephen Biko. Thus, the poem positions Billi Holiday within an African American community that crosses time and brings the past into the present. She names people whose voices functioned as a political force to resist oppression. Gusset's poem moves to focus on the song "Gloomy Sunday" that Billi Holiday adapted, describing how it had such impact that it was believed that some of those who heard it committed suicide, and so it had to be taken off the radio. Gossett questions how Billi Holiday could create something so powerful, asking, "how did she do it and what did she do when she made this record that i am listening to now on this tape that had those bigtime bigdaddies jumping outta windows and otherwise offing theyselves that time" (109). The poet imagines asking Billi for lessons because she knows "some other sisters that want to learn how to use their voices the same way billie did on this record" (111). She sees Billi Holiday as a woman whose power fills the community and whose voice can inspire others to use their own voice. This poem can invite conversation about the political power of music and how it participates in a community of voices.

In the poem, "Zai El-Hawa," we again encounter a singer who exists within a community. Mattawa begins the poem with a picture of an unnamed singer in Paris. The singer buys a shirt, anticipates recording a new song, and playing two concerts. But beneath that is his illness with a reference to "his liver eaten up by bilharzia" (60). The title of the poem and the mention of bilharzia is enough for those readers who know to recognize the man as Abd el Halim Hafez, the famous Egyptian singer. Yet, he remains unnamed throughout the poem, perhaps suggesting the way his own identity becomes subsumed by his audience. The second stanza refers to the poet's cousin who jumped from a balcony the day the singer died. Again, for those familiar with the singer, it is known that several people committed suicide after Abd el Halim Hafez's death. The poet plays a tape of the song, which lasts forty minutes. As he listens to the song recorded live, he hears the audience demanding the song be sung again a second time. There is a distance between the reality of the singer's difficult upbringing that he has kept hidden and the audience who only knows that he had a humble beginning. The audience has placed their emotions onto him, "the kind of man who would end up drunk late that night telling the singer 'I memorize all your songs,' and weep to him about his exile and nostalgia and weep and weep" (61). The poem suggests that the singer internalizes his audience's pain along with his own as he sings, and that is why they demand to hear it again and again. This poem can allow for a discussion about the role of the singer as an iconic figure who articulates the emotions of an entire community.

In the poem, "the hotel worker," Anderson takes the single moment of a hotel worker who stops by drummers on the street and puts a few coins "in Pepe's crocheted hat" (52) and expands it to reveal the intimate details of each action. As the hotel worker drops the coins into the hat, she becomes part of the music: "She sprinkles the coins/She rains them down/She flicks her wrist/makes the music her own" (52). Anderson notes that this woman hears something in the drumming that others only pass by "(a crowd snakes through the scene)" (52). When the woman stops, she shares in the community of this moment with the drummers. The poem ends with an italicized refrain, bringing in the words like a song, "and when she smiles/She gives it back to us" (52). There is an exchange here that surpasses the monetary gift, as the woman has become part of the community of drummers giving something of herself to their music. This poem can initiate a conversation about how both musicians and listeners come together to create community.

Encounters

Write About an Encounter with Someone of a Different Culture

Encountering someone from a different culture can highlight our own cultural identity, and it can also challenge us. We are forced to question who we are in relation to others who have different beliefs, values, and ways of living in the world. It offers an opportunity to step outside of ourselves and see the world differently.

There are also times when such encounters shake our sense of identity in a way that challenges our own values. We must decide whether we want to continue to live by those values or if we want to adopt new ones. Such encounters can become a way of stepping into a new world.

Prompt: Write a scene in which a character encounters someone of another culture and must make a decision on how to interact with that person. Consider the ways that character's cultural values are being challenged through the encounter.

Readings: These readings can lead to discussions about how encountering someone of a different culture can open up new ways of seeing ourselves, how it can allow us to step into a new culture, and how it can help us to make connections across different cultures.

The Sun is also a Star by Nicola Yoon

"First Snow" by Khaled Mattawa in *Dinarzad's Children: An Anthology of Contemporary Arab American Fiction*, edited by Pauline Kaldas and Khaled Mattawa

P. Kaldas, *Writing the Multicultural Experience*,
https://doi.org/10.1007/978-3-031-06124-0_9

"Manar of Hama" by Mohja Kahf in *Dinarzad's Children: An Anthology of Contemporary Arab American Fiction*, edited by Pauline Kaldas and Khaled Mattawa

In the young adult novel, *The Sun is also a Star*, Natasha, whose family is from Jamaica, meets Daniel, whose family is from Korea. Their encounter allows them to see their own lives through different eyes. Daniel begins to imagine a life different from the one his parents have planned for him: "But something about Natasha makes me think my life could be extraordinary" (72). Natasha begins to questions her own prejudices: "I guess I assumed he'd be nerdy because he's Asian" (75). Their encounter with one another pushes them to question the idea of fate and begin to create their own futures. This novel can inspire a conversation about how our encounters lead us to question our own assumptions and help us to see alternatives to our life's path.

In "First Snow," Ali is an international student who has encapsulated himself away from American life. Against the intrusions of college life, he maintains his routine of studying and praying. The story takes place on a snowy evening when his next-door neighbor, Donna, is having an end of semester party. She invites him over, telling him she can fix him up with a girl who is also from another country. The noise from the party intrudes on Ali until he begins to wonder, "He tried to imagine what was happening at the party—what did she look like, this Nima?" (364). He is unable to resist the temptation and ultimately goes to the party. This story allows us to explore the ways that young people interact with one another in different cultures.

In "Manar of Hama," we meet Manar a few months after her arrival from Syria where a brutal attack in Hama has killed Manar's entire family. Carrying this trauma with her, she arrives in the U.S. to find herself completely disconnected. Her dislike of the food symbolizes her alienation. It is when she follows a young woman who smells like allspice that she finds a group of people dancing, chanting Arabic phrases, and eating Hummus. They invite her to join them and she says, "It was my first filling meal in this country" (116). This connection extends beyond food. When they ask her where she is from, she says, "When I said Syria, they did not look blank" (116). This encounter begins Manar's journey to finding a sense of home in her new country. This story can create discussion around how we can find points of familiarity in an encounter with those who are different from us.

Write About an Interaction That Shifted Your Sense of Identity

There are those moments in our lives when our interaction with someone creates a significant change for us. We see ourselves and our place in the world differently. Something in us shifts because of that encounter. Perhaps it makes us value something about our identity that we had taken for granted. Perhaps it makes us see our place in the world differently. Perhaps it gives us a new way of defining ourselves.

Sometimes those interactions also make us assess our own prejudices and force us to confront them. We need to consider how we make certain assumptions about others, and this becomes a moment of questioning. Being open to these encounters and allowing them to affect us can challenge and transform us.

Prompt: Write about a significant interaction that causes a shift in the understanding of someone's identity. Consider why this encounter changes things. What assumptions or prejudices are being challenged? How does the encounter affect those ideas? How does the encounter transform the person or the relationship?

Readings: These readings can lead to discussions about how an encounter makes us understand our position in the world differently, how it pushes us to question our prejudices, and how it transforms our sense of identity.

> *The Visitor* directed by Thomas McCarthy
> "News from Phoenix" by Joseph Geha in *Dinarzad's Children*, edited by Pauline
>   Kaldas and Khaled Mattawa
> "Meeting" by Yasmine Anderson, in *Mizna: Prose, Poetry, and Art Exploring
>   Arab America*

The Visitor focuses on the encounter between Walter, an older white professor, and the undocumented immigrants he finds living in his apartment in New York. He develops a friendship with Tarek who teaches him to drum, enabling him to find a way out of the grief over his wife's death and a way to move his stagnant emotional and intellectual life. That encounter is furthered when he meets Tarek's mother after Tarek has been placed in a detention center. Walter's identity as a privileged upper class white man comes into question when he confronts the system set up for undocumented immigrants. In one scene at the detention center when he is unable to receive any information about where Tarek has been taken, he loses his temper, experiencing perhaps for the first time a loss of power. It is ultimately Walter who is transformed in this movie. The movie that can initiate discussions about the various privileges people have, especially by comparing Walter and Tarek.

"News from Phoenix" is a story that shows an encounter between a Lebanese couple and a Jewish couple. Sofia has strong prejudices against Jews and is cautious around the couple while her husband, Amos, has learned to trust Erwin who advises him on financial matters relating to his store. When Erwin's wife, Charlotte, has a miscarriage, Sofia's sense of humanity and prejudice collide with one another, forcing her to reconsider her views, "When Sofia came in, her face was white. ... 'Small as my hand,' she said, 'but perfect'" (95). At the end of the story, her ability to laugh at the prejudices she has been taught becomes a transformative moment for Sofia. This story can create a conversation about the prejudices we hold and what happens when they are confronted with the reality of meeting someone.

The prose poem, "Meeting," relays a scene in a grocery store where the speaker is drawn to a couple speaking in Arabic. She moves toward the watermelons to be closer to them, "fruit my mother taught me to cup in my hand, tapping the emerald shells to find the best one" (3). She considers locating her sister and speaking a few words of Arabic, so that the couple might turn to her in recognition. The poem concludes with "I see now that my mother was not teaching me how to pick the best watermelon, but how to send out a signal in a new language, to call out to a stranger in a grocery store, to say, 'I'm here'" (3). It is the desire to be seen and heard as a member of the Arab community that centers this poem. The poem invites us to consider how an encounter can highlight our sense of cultural identity.

Write About Explaining Your Culture

There are times when we are placed in a position that requires us to explain our culture. We have to find ways to explain what is natural for us to those who are unfamiliar with it. The awkward nature of this interaction can highlight our feelings of being an outsider. Having to offer an explanation of a cultural ritual reminds us that we do not belong in the mainstream of society.

The anticipation of how someone will respond to our explanation creates tension in such a situation. Will they welcome the information we provide or ridicule it? How will this affect the way we are perceived by others? These cultural encounters can become moments of tension or connection.

Prompt: Write about a time when you had to explain an aspect of your culture to someone else or create a scene when a character is in this situation.

Consider your own feelings as you are placed in the situation of having to explain and recount the other person's reaction and its impact on you.

Readings: These readings can lead to discussions about how we acquire the role of explainer, how we anticipate the reaction of others to our explanation, and how having to explain our culture can make us see it differently.

The House on Mango Street by Sandra Cisneros
The Sun is also a Star by Nicola Yoon
"My Father and the Figtree" in *Words Under the Words* by Naomi Shihab Nye

In the vignette, "Papa Who Wakes Up Tired in the Dark," Esperanza's father tells her that her grandfather in Mexico has died. As the eldest child who understands the cultural rituals, she becomes the one who must explain them to her siblings, so she will "have to explain why we can't play. I will have to tell them to be quiet today" (56–57). Esperanza's tone in this vignette shows that she understands the burden of this responsibility. This vignette can invite a conversation about how the role of cultural explainer can be carried by certain members of the family.

In one scene in *The Sun is also a Star*, Natasha and Daniel go to eat at a Korean restaurant. Daniel is on edge as he anticipates Natasha's response to the food: "A part of me braces to have to explain to her what she's eating. Once, a friend made a *What's in this food? Is it dog?* Joke. I felt like shit but I still laughed" (156). However, Natasha's response shows that the two of them will be able to embrace their cultural differences when she says, "This is delicious" and does not ask for an explanation (157). This becomes a moment of sharing culture with complete acceptance. This scene can raise issues about how the request for an explanation can affect a relationship.

In the poem, "My Father and the Fig Tree," Nye recounts a series of interactions with her father as he tries to explain the value of figs. Initially, her father places figs in every story he tells her. When she eats a dried fig, he has to explain, "That's not what I'm talking about!" (20). In the last stanza, her father sings a song that she is unable to understand until he tells her, "It's a figtree song" and shows her the fig tree he has planted. She finally understands when she sees him "plucking his fruits like ripe tokens,/emblems, assurance/of a world that was always his own" (21). She knows that the figs represent the world of Palestine that her father has lost and that he has been trying to pass on to her. This poem can create conversations about how parents or older relatives pass on and explain their culture to their children.

Write About Microaggressions

The microaggressions we experience in our daily life accumulate in subtle ways. While a single incident might be brushed off as ignorant or unintentional, the constant deluge of such actions takes a toll, often making us feel that we must be constantly on guard. They accumulate in multiple layers, making our school or our workplace hostile. Microaggressions can be unintentional on the part of the person who commits them, but they reveal the layers of racism and prejudice that exist in our society. Comments such as *You speak English so well* or *You must be good at basketball* make assumptions about a person before actually getting to know them as an individual. Other comments such as referring to a person who speaks with an accent as "unintelligible" can be more insidious and damaging. Bringing these microaggressions to light and exposing them so they can be investigated in terms of their source as well as their impact makes visible the constant sense of oppression that diverse people experience in their daily lives.

Shortly after I arrived in the U.S., my classmates asked me questions such as "Did you live in the pyramids?" and "Did you own a camel?" The questions were so absurd to me that I did not bother to answer. Looking back, I now understand how these comments turned me into a quiet person reluctant to share any information about myself. As an adult, I sometimes get a different version of those same comments when the first question someone asks after they learn that I am from Egypt is "Have you seen the pyramids?" There are myriad ways that we experience these types of microaggressions, and they continue to be a constant part of our lives.

Prompt: Recall a time when you experienced a microaggression related to your identity. Write the scene of that experience. Try writing in present tense to evoke the immediacy of the experience. Recall as many details as you can to amplify that moment and make it visible. You could stop there and let the scene stand on its own or you might continue and bring in your reflective voice to consider the implications of that interaction, the intention, your response, its impact, and how it may have changed for you.

Readings: These readings can lead to discussions about the source of microaggressions, how they impact our sense of self, and how we respond to them.

"The Myth of the Latin Woman: I Just Met a Girl Named Maria" in *The Latin Deli* by Judith Ortiz Cofer

The Four Immigrant Manga by Henry (Yoshitaka) Kiyama

"To the Man Who Shouted 'I Like Pork Fried Rice' at Me on the Street" in *Floating, Brilliant, Gone* by Franny Choi

In "The Myth of the Latin Woman: I Just Met a Girl Named Maria," Judith Ortiz Cofer recalls giving her first reading. When she enters the restaurant where she is reading, a woman sitting at a table asks her to bring her a cup of coffee, assuming she is a waitress. The interaction makes her realize what she has to "overcome before anyone would take me seriously" (153). As she reads her work, she singles out that woman: "That day I read to that woman and her lowered eyes told me that she was embarrassed at her little faux pas. And when I willed her to look up at me, it was my victory" (153). Ortiz Cofer responds to this microaggression by claiming her place on the stage. This essay can invite discussion about how we choose to respond to microaggressions.

In Episode 11 of *The Four Immigrant Manga*, a woman who is looking for someone to clean her home stops a man on the street and says, "You are a nice clean looking Jap boy. … Come and work for me" (51). When he responds, "I am not such a domestic labor. But I am consul of Empire," she says, "But your looks like my laundry boy" (51). Her response demeans him, indicating that because of his appearance, he is only capable of being a domestic laborer who can serve her. This microaggression gives us a glimpse into how the Japanese were treated as having lesser abilities and intelligence. This episode can raise issues about the connection between stereotypes and microaggressions.

In the poem, "To the Man Who Shouted 'I Like Pork Fried Rice' at Me on the Street," Franny Choi dissects the man's comment, critiquing how this man views her. In lines like "you candid cannibal./you want me bite-sized/no eyes clogging your throat," (38) she reveals how she is viewed as something to be consumed. Ultimately, the poet refuses to be seen through this man's eyes and says, "[W]atch me kick back to life. watch me tentacles/& teeth. watch me/ resurrected electric" (39). In response to this microaggression, Choi exacts her revenge through the poem. This poem can open up a conversation about the power of words and how writing can be a response to microaggressions.

Write an Argument in Dialogue Focusing on Culture

Dialogue is a powerful tool for writers. It brings characters to life through their voices and actions, and it gives momentum to any piece of writing. When that dialogue is an argument, it highlights the tension of the piece and reveals what is at stake. In setting up an argument, it's important to give attention to setting, movement, gestures, and facial expression, so that the dialogue works as a scene that can be imagined by the reader.

Arguments that focus on culture highlight the tensions surrounding how we negotiate our identities and our relationship to each other. They can bring out the inner emotions of a character, their fears, and the sense of precariousness they feel about their position in the world. They can also highlight the different perspectives two people have about each other's culture.

Prompt: Write an argument between two people that focuses on culture, highlighting the tension surrounding the topic. Give special attention to gestures, tone of voice, and facial expression to reveal how communication happens in non-verbal ways.

Readings: These readings lead to discussion about arguments regarding cultural behavior, cultural practices, and perceptions of home.

> "Confessions" by Amy Tan in *Short Takes: Brief Encounters with Contemporary Nonfiction*, edited by Judith Kitchen.
> "Stage Directions for an Extended Conversation" by Yussef El Guindi in *Dinarzad's Children: An Anthology of Contemporary Arab American Fiction*, edited by Pauline Kaldas and Khaled Mattawa
> "A Conversation" in *The Time Between Places* by Pauline Kaldas

In Amy Tan's essay, "Confessions," mother and daughter argue in the confines of a small chalet in the Alps where they have moved from China. The argument centers on the daughter having a boyfriend. What makes this argument interesting is the way in which the daughter responds to the mother's angry words with movement and gestures rather than speaking. When her mother says, "Stop seeing him!" Tan says, "I shook my head" (89). That gesture carries more power than if she had said no as it is uttered through her body's movement. And when her mother accuses her of not being sad when her father and brother died, Tan says, "I kept my face to the window, unmoved" (89). That action speaks to her desire to escape from her mother's emotional entrapment and a refusal to engage. The argument culminates when her mother, seeking some reaction from her, appears with a meat cleaver, threatening to kill her. When the daughter finally speaks and says, "I want to live," (90) the tension of the moment is broken and the connection between mother and daughter is reestablished. This essay offers ideas for how disagreements are communicated in verbal and non-verbal ways.

In "Stage Directions for an Extended Conversation," El Guindi, who is a playwright, gives us an uncomfortable interaction between an Egyptian man and an American woman after they have just watched a documentary about female circumcision in an Egyptian Village. As the woman questions the man about the practice, it is clear that this argument has more to do with the power dynamics in their relationship. While the man agrees with her that the practice is hideous, he is unwilling to say so, "This was about staking a moral claim as their relationship naturally entered its next, post-glow phase" (185). He avoids her questions as they negotiate this argument through conversation, silences, and actions. This story can initiate a discussion about how arguments about different cultural practices can be a focus for personal conflicts.

The story, "A Conversation," takes place completely through dialogue, but that dialogue exists on two levels. The words in quotes are those spoken aloud by each character, and the words below the quotes are the character's inner thoughts. In this way, two layers of communication happen simultaneously. As the couple argue over whether to remain in the U.S. or to return to Egypt, we see how their memories of Egypt and their experiences in the U.S. have shaped their view on where they want to live for the remainder of their life. At one point, the husband says, "You can have everything there. I'll buy you whatever you want" (114). Beneath his verbal promise of wealth in Egypt is his inner voice that recalls the struggles they faced when they arrived in America, "Those first years, every penny we had to hold tight in our fists. ... Every birthday I failed you, and even a single rose was an extravagance I held back" (114). In this way, the inner thoughts reveal both the memory and desire that motivates each person's reasons for remaining in America or returning to Egypt. This story can invite an exploration of what lies beneath the verbal arguments that take place between people.

Write About Travel

Travel experiences have been written about in various ways. One of the problems with travel writing occurs when place and culture are being viewed through the outsider's gaze. When that gaze takes on the voice of authority and knowledge, the result often presents a limited and inaccurate view. When we travel, we take who we are with us, and we must recognize that our vision is limited by our knowledge and upbringing. Writing from our perspective with that awareness can lead to a more honest portrayal of our travels and their significance. Wherever we are feels like the center, and the great advantage of travel is that we shift that center, allowing us to see the world and ourselves from a different perspective.

When I return to Egypt, I am often asked for the first week or so where I am from. While people often assume I'm from an Arab country, something about me seems a little off. Within two weeks, the questions stop, and I am perceived as Egyptian. My body and my language re-adapt, and I can once again belong. Our identities shift as we travel to new places. When my husband and I went to Zimbabwe in 1990, we were assumed to be South African. It did not occur to anyone that we might be American. These shifts in perceptions allow for new insights into our identities and the places where we reside.

Prompt: As you approach this prompt, you might begin by making a list of the places where you have traveled. It would be good to set this up as a timeline, adding the year, your age, and who traveled with you. This is a subject that lends itself to writing short scenes, recalling specific experiences from your trip. Give attention to the place as well as how you positioned yourself and how you might have been perceived by others. As you continue, consider how the experience transformed you and your sense of identity.

Readings: These readings can lead to discussions about how our perception of homeland changes when we travel, how we shift our understanding of what is normal, and how our values are challenged.

> *The Language of Baklava,* by Diana Abu Jaber
> *Sitti's Secrets* by Naomi Shihab Nye
> *The Farewell,* directed by Lulu Wang

In the chapter, "Native Foods," from Diana Abu Jaber's memoir, *The Language of Baklava,* we watch as Diana travels to Jordan with her family and remains there for a year. Her cultural negotiations are reflected in the childhood friendships she makes and unmakes as she tries to figure out where she belongs. As she adapts and learns the language, she says, "It's as if there's only a certain amount of space in my brain, and the more space Jordan takes up, the less room there is left for America" (58). Her time in Jordan remains with her even as she returns to the U.S., and she eventually decides to return for another extended visit. This memoir can offer an opportunity for discussion about how travel changes our sense of identity and the community to which we belong.

Sitti's Secrets is a picture book that tells the beautiful story of a young girl going to visit her grandmother in Palestine. She learns how to communicate with her despite their language differences and begins to understand her life and the values by which she lives. "Soon we had invented our own language together. Sitti pointed at my stomach to ask if I was hungry. I pointed to the door to ask if she wanted to go outside." That understanding also expands the girl's political awareness of the precarious life of those who live in Palestine. This picture book can raise issues about how travel and connection with other people can give us a wider view of the world.

The Farewell is a movie that portrays the experiences of Billi, a young woman who goes to visit her grandmother in Hong Kong. The grandmother has been diagnosed with cancer, and the family chooses not to tell her about the diagnosis. Instead, the whole family travels to Hong Kong to be with her before she dies. This trip causes Billi to struggle as she tries to make sense of her family's decision to deceive her grandmother. When her uncle tells her that the lie allows the family to carry the burden for the grandmother, Billi begins to gain an understanding of the difference between the individualistic culture of the U.S. and her more communal culture. This movie can invite a conversation about how traveling into another culture can enable us to understand the different ways we support one another within a community.

Inheritance

Write About the First Stories You Were Told

What inspires us to write? Where does the movement toward language, story-telling, and the rhythm of words come from? Why does one person gravitate toward music or dance or painting? How does our journey to becoming a certain kind of artist begin? Recalling the first stories we were told can help us excavate the origins of our desire to write. For me, it was my grandmother sitting on my bed as I fell asleep and telling me stories from the Bible. She did not read them but told them as stories—Joseph and the Coat of Many Colors is the one I remember most clearly. These stories were full of vivid characters, intrigue, and conflict, inspiring my imagination. The first books I read when I came to America were fairytales, and I realize now that it was a natural movement—something in those fairytales must have reminded me of the stories my grandmother told me.

The first stories we hear do not affect us only through their narrative but also through the context in which they are being told and the person telling them. Hearing these first stories as I was falling asleep allowed them to become even more embellished by the power of my dreaming. That it was my grandmother, the person I was closest to as a child, who told them to me created the association of love with storytelling.

Prompt: Think back to the first stories you were told, to your first experience with how language could turn into narrative, poetry, music, voice, and create an entrance into another world. Paint the scene of that first experience and move back into it to see what you can discover about the origins of your desire to write.

P. Kaldas, *Writing the Multicultural Experience*,
https://doi.org/10.1007/978-3-031-06124-0_10

Readings: These readings can lead to discussions about the stories we carry from our childhood, the origin stories of our culture, and those who inspired our love of reading and writing.

> *The Map of Salt and Stars* by Zeyn Joukhadar
> *The First Strawberries* by Joseph Bruchac
> "My Rosetta" in *Woman in Front of the Sun* by Judith Ortiz Cofer

In *The Map of Salt and Stars*, the young narrator, Nour, tells the story of her family leaving Syria after their home has been destroyed. As they make their way across several countries to find safety, Nour recalls her favorite story of Rawiya, who in the twelfth century was apprenticed to a map maker and made her way along the same path that Nour's family is now taking. The two stories intertwine with each other, creating a larger story of survival as both girls must disguise themselves as boys in order to make their journey. The story of Rawiya was initially told to her by her father: "The winter before Baba went into the earth, he never missed a bedtime story. ... Baba made my favorite one, the story of the mapmaker's apprentice, last two whole months. ... When he lost his voice, I told the ending. Then the story was ours" (5). As she tells the story, "the words come back like they had never left, like it had been me telling the story all along" (6). Telling the story of Rawiya allows Nour to find her own strength as she moves from place to place. This book can enable us to explore how those early stories from our culture shape our own identity and guide us.

The First Strawberries is based on a Cherokee story and is retold in this picture book. The story begins with equality between man and woman. That equality threatens to break when the man reprimands the woman for not having prepared his meal. The woman responds, "Your words hurt me. ... I will live with you no longer." The couple must find a way to move toward healing. It is only when the man recognizes that he "was foolish to speak angry words" and asks the woman for her forgiveness that they are able to regain their relationship. This picture book can make us consider the creation stories we were taught and how they portray the relationship between men and women.

"My Rosetta" recalls Ortiz Cofer's first mentor who widened her reading from romance stories to the larger world of literature. When Sister Rosetta discovers her reading a trashy romance novel, she offers her an alternative reading list. "The next week she handed me a paper sack containing *Women in Love*, *Madame Bovary*, and *Wuthering Heights*. ... I had begun to read a page for the effect the words had on me rather than just for the juicy parts. ... Sister Rosetta's was a reading list without apparent order, but it all came together inside me" (8–9). Ortiz Cofer learns about great literature and also about the power of language. This essay can invite conversation about those who introduced us to the first books we read and how they influenced our desire to write.

Write About Your Origins

Writing about your origins opens a wide arena—the people you come from, the place, the culture. Where and from whom do you come? How do you trace yourself back? How do you define your lineage to know who you are today?

My origins take me back to my family, which I can trace back three generations, and it takes me to place, which is not only the city of Cairo but also the villages where both sides of my family originated. For me, the question becomes how to carry this with me, especially while living in the U.S.

Prompt: This prompt is an opportunity to consider what and who generated your presence in the world. If you move in the direction of people, the questions might be: Where did they come from? What did they carry with them? How did their definition of who they are influence you? If you think of place, consider where that place is in your life—A nostalgic memory? Loss? Desire? How does place provide identity? If it is culture, was that culture subsumed for the sake of assimilation or was it passed on in visible or perhaps invisible ways? Writing becomes a way to explore those origins, to allow the breath of their existence to live on the page.

Readings: These readings can lead to discussions about the stories we tell about where we come from, the way we learn about our past, and the larger histories that have shaped us.

> *Caucasia* by Danzy Senna
> "American Arithmetic" in *Postcolonial Love Poem* by Natalie Diaz
> "The Declension of History in the Key of If" by M. Nourbese Philip in *Letters to the Future: Black Women Radical Writing*, edited by Erica Hunt and Dawn Lundy Martine

Caucasia explores how the main character, Birdie, loses her origins. From the beginning, her physical appearance separates her from her Black father, her culture, and ultimately from her sister. Birdie's Blackness comes into question because her appearance is not perceived as Black, marking her as an outsider to the race. Her journey becomes one of loss and re-discovery as the family is split across racial lines with her sister, Cole, staying with their Black father and Birdie going with their white mother. As she and her mother create new identities for themselves, her mother also creates a new origin for Birdie: "We're gonna need to use our imaginations. You know, make up a history for you. … I was knighted a half-Jewish girl named Jesse Goldman, with a white mama named Sheila" (130–131). Hiding her Blackness is presented to her as an act of survival and a way to protect her mother. While her physical appearance allows her to make her Blackness invisible, it is her new life story that pulls the cloak fully over her identity. Birdie's origins become further removed from her, causing a kind of disassociation to occur. This book can raise issues about what happens when we keep the story of our origins and identity hidden from others.

Natalie Diaz's poem, "American Arithmetic," looks at origins through the lens of what has been lost. The poem begins with the statistic of how few Native Americans exist today, highlighting the destruction of Indigenous peoples: "Native Americans make up less than/1 percent of the population of America" (17). This loss makes the past an inaccessible memory for the poet, "I do not remember the days before America—/I do not remember the days when we were all here" (17). The poem moves to the present and the way Native Americans are killed by the police, continuing their destruction. The poet struggles against the past and present destruction of her people. Referring to the National Museum of the American Indian, the poet says, "I am doing my best not to become a museum," (17) a plea against complete disappearance that continues with "Let me be lonely but not invisible" (18). It is an attempt to hold on to the existence not only of herself but of her people and their origins. This poem invites conversation about the loss of origins and how one can resist that loss.

In her poetic essay, "The Declension of History in the Key of If," M. Nourbese Philip interrogates the past through the use of parts of speech, especially verb tenses. Her exploration of memory and history with a focus on the Caribbean is an attempt to understand her own origins. "West Indian or Caribbean history was not taught in schools until the sixties. Until then our history was British history. Indeed we were told that we didn't have a history. We were loyal subjects of the empire—descendants of nameless, placeless slaves" (298). For Philip, the passage of time cannot be neatly divided but exists simultaneously. "The past, present and future are, however, in dynamic relationship invigorating or bleeding into each other as the case may be" (300). Philip excavates the history of slavery in the Caribbean and the way it continues to be carried through memory and place. She imagines the history and the people who brought her to this place "to confront the memory of my missing history and the history of my absent memory" (311). She shows how the history of slavery resulted in the loss of culture, language, history, family. This piece can motivate a discussion about how we can see our origins through historical and political events.

Write About Returning to Homeland

Returning to a homeland—whether it is the place where we were born or a place that we only know through the stories from our family—is an experience that shifts our sense of identity and belonging. If we lived in our homeland for part of our upbringing then we have memories that we carry with us. Depending on our experiences, our memories might be filled with the nostalgia of our childhood. If we know our homeland only through the stories of our family, that homeland may feel distant and removed from our experiences. If we feel a deep sense of separation in the country where we live, we might imagine our homeland as a place where we will fully belong.

When I returned to live and work in Egypt for a period of three years, my childhood nostalgia was confronted with a country struggling with class inequality and political turmoil. I also discovered that I both belonged and didn't belong in my homeland. Having lived away from it for so long, I existed in a liminal place.

Prompt: Write about a time when you returned to your homeland or write about a character who returns to their homeland. Consider the history of the person returning and the way they imagine their homeland. Go further to describe either your own experience of returning or a character's return. How do the expectations collide with the reality? How does the experience affect the person's sense of identity?

Readings: These readings can lead to discussions about what we carry with us when we return to our homeland, the anxieties we may have about returning, and the precarious experience of having multiple national affiliations.

> *Behold the Dreamers* by Imbolo Mbue
> *The Other Half of Happy* by Rebecca Balcárcel
> "Repatriation: A Libya Memoir" by Khaled Mattawa in *Beyond Memory: An Anthology of Contemporary Arab American Creative Nonfiction*, edited by Pauline Kaldas and Khaled Mattawa

Behold the Dreamers ends as Jende and Neni are preparing to return to Cameroon. For them, Cameroon has been a place of no opportunities where they could not succeed. Now they return, carrying with them their failed American dream with the anticipation of making that dream come true in Cameroon. Neni takes the clothes given to her by the wealthy woman for whom she worked as a way to gain status: "she was now a woman of class, with real designer items, and none of them could compete with her" (381). Jende takes with him an idea for starting his own business so he can have the status and wealth of the man for whom he worked as a chauffeur: "He was going to be a businessman. He would get a nice brick house for them" (350). Their vision of their homeland has been transformed into a place where they can fulfill the American dream. This novel can bring up thoughts about how we carry our dreams from one place to another and how our vision of our homeland changes after we have been away from it.

Throughout *The Other Half of Happy*, Quijana is fearful of the trip her parents have planned to Guatemala, her father's country of birth. She feels unable to meet her father's expectations to be Guatemalan. Her inadequate knowledge of Spanish, her lack of interest in her father's music, and her inability to communicate with her Guatemalan grandmother make her "wish there was no Guatemala. No place that would ever make me feel stupid and not-good-enough" (66). When she does go at the end, her fears dissipate as she realizes that she is fully embraced by her Guatemalan family and that it is possible to communicate without language. When she meets her grandmother, she says, "[H]er eyes pour love into mine. ... I can see that words don't matter as much as I thought" (316). This novel can be a way to consider the fears that accompany a return to homeland.

In "Repatriation: A Libya Memoir," Mattawa takes us on his journey back to Libya to attend his father's funeral after living in the U.S. for twenty-one years. He begins with the awareness "that the official Libyan ID I've been carrying was just a receipt and not the real thing," (173) thus placing himself in a kind of identity limbo that continues throughout the essay. When his father dies in Germany and they prepare to take his body back to Libya, Mattawa decides to return. Making arrangements to go to Libya requires the retrieval of both his Libyan and American passports, once again marking his shifting national identity by his documentation. Once he finally returns, he exists both on the inside and outside of the culture. "At the wake, I shook hands with two thousand men. I saw relatives I'd not seen since childhood. ... I stared at every passerby and through every half-opened door, soaking up the strange familiarity, reintroducing my face to the old neighborhood" (183–184). The phrase "strange familiarity" captures his experience as he attempts to re-enter the culture through family and place. At the end, he explains that the Libyan identity card and the American passport have the same photo, saying,

"Seeing my face on both documents together for the first time suggested that I was somehow able to outfox both nations, and that I had found a sense of autonomy that transcended exile and belonging" (184). While this appears as an assertion, it actually reinforces his feelings of exile and unbelonging as he has to manipulate a system of documentation to be able to move from one identity/nation to another. This essay can invite conversation about the intersection of identity, documentation, and national identity.

Write About Superstitions

In many cultures, superstitions are an integral part of daily life. Certain beliefs are woven into the fabric of how we live: don't sweep at night; knock on wood to bring good luck; throw salt over your shoulder if you spill it; don't walk under ladders; if your left hand itches, you'll gain money; if your right hand itches, you'll lose money. If we learn certain superstitions from a young age, they become integrated into our life without stopping to think about them.

Considering the influence of superstitions on our life can open a door to a greater awareness of cultural beliefs and how they get passed on. What values are embedded in each superstition? How do superstitions relate to a culture's ideas about fate, about good and evil, and about control over our own lives?

Prompt: This is an opportunity to think about the role of superstitions in your life or you can create a character where superstitions impact their life choices. Make a list of superstitions that have been passed on to you and then highlight the ones you actually follow. Consider how they affect your perception of your life and the decisions you make.

Readings: These readings can lead to discussion about how certain aspects of language reflect cultural beliefs, how superstitions differ among cultures, and how superstitions affect our behaviors.

"Insha'Allah" in *The Moons of August* by Danusha Laméris
"Superstition" in *Say I Won't* by Ashley August
"An Evening Sweep: 1998" in *Letters from Cairo* by Pauline Kaldas

In the poem, "Insha'Allah," Laméris recounts how the word "Insha'Allah" has entered her speech, so it follows each time she articulates a plan for the future. She considers how this word has been used throughout the generations and especially by mothers who have held onto hope: "*Our sons will return next month, insha'Allah./Insha'Allah, this war will end soon. Insha'Allah/the rice will be enough to last through winter*" (19). The phrase transforms in the poem from its literal meaning of "if God wills it" to an expression of hope uttered by women. This poem inspires discussion around how certain superstitions/beliefs are embedded in our language.

"Superstition" begins with an explanation of how whistling indoors in Central America is believed to bring in bad luck: "It meant you were asking for your home to be set on fire from the foundation" (1). The poem shifts to how whistling is common in America and done in various places. While the poet learns how to whistle, she only does so outdoors. The poem expresses her fear "of meeting the person who will ruin me by whistling" (1). Her fear is linked to her worry of not obeying her mother and allowing ghosts to enter her life, linking the superstition of whistling with ghosts. This poem invites conversation about what happens when there are cultural differences around superstitions.

In "An Evening Sweep," I recount our hope of finding jobs and making a move as my husband and I finish our graduate program. The superstition I had learned was "If you sweep (or vacuum—we had to adjust it to include the new technology once we arrived in America) at night, then you will move" (149). The essay explores the possible origins of this belief, relating it to the fact that moving is not viewed positively in Egypt. When a couple marries, they set up their apartment and they stay there permanently. Moves tend to happen because of difficult circumstances, such as someone's death or immigration. Taking this superstition, I turn it around and sweep at night in the hope of moving: "Apparently I had only reversed the sweeping one, attempting to manipulate it to my own desires by sweeping at night so that we would move" (149–150). My attempt to manipulate the superstition highlights my position between two cultures, as sweeping at night with the hope of moving reflects a desire to "reach home" (152). This essay allows us to explore how we carry superstitions from one place to another.

Write from a Photograph or a Series of Photographs

Most homes have photo albums or boxes of photos tucked away. These photos tell the stories of our past and our family's past. Pictures of weddings, birthdays, baptisms, trips—they are the past carried into the future. Excavating these photos becomes a way of entering into the past and has the potential to open conversations with other family members as they identify the people and places in those photos. It can be a way of tracing ourselves back, and it can also be a way of seeing the progression of our lives. When those pictures come from another country, they open a door into that world.

The photographs I carry are the ones that were taken the day before we immigrated when our whole family came to our home and we took several pictures. When I look at them, I remember everyone and everything from those first years of my life. I can identify each family member and trace their own life journey, those who also immigrated and those who stayed. These photos hold our lives still before our immigration changed everything.

Prompt: Find an old photograph or a series of photographs. If possible, ask someone about the photos: who is in them and where they were taken. Write about what these photos reveal. Consider what you know and don't know from these pictures. How do they make you see your life differently?

Readings: These readings can lead to discussions about the way photographs document history, the significance of holding on to certain photographs, and the stories behind a series of photographs.

> *Desert Exile* by Yoshiko Uchida
> *Arabian Jazz* by Diana Abu Jaber
> "Part One and Part Two: A Place Without Question" by Celine Anderson in *Dardishi*

In *Desert Exile*, Uchida includes several photographs of the internment camps where her family lived. Given that the history of the Japanese internment is rarely taught in the schools and that it remains an invisible part of American history, these photos serve as tangible evidence of the camps. While Uchida describes the conditions under which her family lived, the photos serve as a visual document. In one photograph, we see a picture of the horse stalls where her family lived in the Tanforan camp (73). For most readers, it would be difficult to imagine living in this type of structure without the photo. By including photos of her family in the camps, Uchida brings the internment experience to life in a way that also removes the dehumanization of the Japanese that took place during this time. This aspect of the book can open up possibilities for how to bring photos and text together to create a narrative.

In one scene of *Arabian Jazz*, the younger daughter, Melvina, pulls out a photo album that she has kept for herself. She was only two when her mother died, and as she opens the album, she expects it to reveal some hidden truth about their mother, using those photos to compensate for her loss. "At the top of the page there was a photograph of Matussem, Jemorah, and her mother, grandly pregnant. ... The images were amorphous, eerily distinct" (193). As

Melvina and her sister look at the photographs, Melvina closes the album, saying, "The pictures are too solid, they get in the way, they crowd out … what I have left of her" (194–195). It is Jemorah and Melvina's recognition that their mother looks like them that reveals some truth from the photographs—that they are their mother's daughters, and although she is gone, they remain connected to her. This scene enables us to consider how photos can allow us to access the past and bring that past into our present moment.

In the two parts of "A Place Without Question," my daughter, Celine Anderson, took several old photographs and created a photo essay/interview. She begins by explaining, "My mom and I found an old shoebox full of photographs from their first few years in the States." From those photographs, she selected several around which to build her piece. The photos are interspersed with the interview she did with me, recounting our immigration and early years in the U.S. While she does not specifically discuss the photos, she interweaves them throughout the piece, so they become part of the story. The captions beneath identify not only the people in the photo but also the time and place. For one photo, she writes that it included my parents and I "*Sitting in a bedroom of their Mohandessin apartment the night before they immigrated. December 1969*," marking the importance of time and place. In this way, she creates a layered immigrant narrative made of her own observations and questions, my responses to those questions, and the photos which give the story a visual dimension. As she says, "These pictures are from the early 70's, a time sans social media, when photos were not necessarily taken with the intent of *showing* but *remembering*. I like to think of these as visual insurance of my family's previous life." This is a good piece for discussing how a series of photos can be used to tell a larger story.

Write a Letter/Poem Addressed to Children

Inheritance is not only about what we inherit but also about what we pass on to the next generation. What do we hope that generation will carry from us? Do we want to pass on language, recipes, traditions, family history, and values? The research being done on generational trauma shows that we pass on some things unknowingly through our genes. In a sense, each of us holds the experiences of our ancestors. Other things we pass on more consciously, and some things we pass on through the example of how we live, like traditions and values. As people of different cultures marry and have children, there is a fear of losing some of our cultural beliefs and practices, so at times those things must be passed on more purposefully.

The next generation may not always be biological children. There may be nieces, nephews, and other younger members in your family to whom you wish to pass on something. It is also valuable to imagine the children that do not yet exist and consider what you might want to give them. Imagining that legacy allows us to see far into the future, to see beyond ourselves.

Prompt: If you have children, write to those children; if not, consider writing to your unborn children. You can also write to a child within your family. You might want to write this in the form of a letter or a poem dedicated to that child. Consider what you want to give them, what you want them to continue holding in their own lives.

Readings: These readings can lead to discussions about the things we want to pass on to the next generation.

"ABC/Alif Beh Teh" in *Egyptian Compass* by Pauline Kaldas
"An Alphabet for My Daughters" in *River to Cross* by T. J. Anderson III
"Origins" in *Geographies of Light* by Lisa Suhair Majaj

I wrote the poem, "ABC/Alif Beh Teh" when I was twenty-six, six years before I had my first daughter. At the time, it was written to my imaginary children. After my daughters were born, I dedicated the poem to them. Even before their existence, I could imagine them. The poem's title with the first three letters of both the English and the Arabic alphabet speaks to the awareness that my children will live inside both of these worlds. Each piece of the poem is marked by an Arabic letter, guiding the child to enter their world through a language that might be lost. It is the fear of that loss that motivates the poem as the children are asked to remember their ancestors, "like your great grandmother's face melting into the sweat," their immigrant history that brought them to America, "as your grandparents choked their last/Arabic signature bought/you a ticket to America," and the language, "in the center below your heart/pull to a tone like a cymbal" (15). In this way, the poem becomes a passing on of the past that might get lost in the alphabet of the new language. This poem can motivate discussion about the importance of passing on family history to our children.

When my husband wrote the poem, "An Alphabet for My Daughters," he also chose the alphabet to direct the movement of the poem. I suspect both of us were thinking about the way language allows us to enter into an understanding of our world and express ourselves. Written in couplets, this poem makes its way through the alphabet, offering the poet's daughters items from each letter. While the English alphabet is used, it is important to recognize the cultural relevance of some of the items, such as "deltas of cowry shells," "lecterns of Kente cloth," and "urns of tamarind brown" (93–94). These offerings connect the daughters to a cultural ancestry grounded in African and African American culture. This poem can invite a conversation about how we imagine passing on our cultural heritage to our children.

"Origins" recalls the birth of Majaj's daughter with images of travel. The child's entrance into the world is marked by the cultural reference of music: "She came headfirst into a space of music, Fairuz singing *Jerusalem in My Heart*" (14). These lines reference Lebanon where Fairuz is from and Palestine, two countries that connect the child to her Arab origins. The poet is asked if she wishes her child to belong to a particular place: "do I hope she will one day return to Palestine, to the United States, to Cyprus, to any of her points of origin?" (14). In response, the poet hopes for her child a place of "her own whole heart," (14) resisting these geographical boundaries. This poem can enable us to explore how we pass on culture to our children when their own identity encompasses multiple locations.

Resistance

Write About Obstacles/Limitations/Restrictions

The obstacles we encounter in our life might be related to our race/ethnicity, our class, our family's expectations, our immigrant status, or our own internal struggle. Thinking of the ways our various identities result in limitations becomes a process of exploration to unearth the foundation of those limitations. Exploring how aspects of our identity lead to restrictions that impact our ability to live fully in our particular location can be a way of making visible those things that inhibit our lives.

When we first arrived in the U.S., it quickly became apparent that my knowledge of English was insufficient. People spoke quickly with an American accent and used slang that was different from the British English I had learned in my school in Egypt. The inability to speak and understand this English held me back for a year in fourth grade, affecting my process of adapting to my new country and succeeding within the school system.

Prompt: Make a list of the obstacles/limitations/restrictions that you experience in your life, especially those that are related to identity and culture. Select one to explore more fully. Think of a particular example when you felt the pressure of that limitation. Consider how it impacts the choices you make, how it might inhibit the way you live, and the goals you set for yourself.

Readings: These readings can lead to discussions about restrictions based on culture, gender, and race.

> *Wadjda* directed by Haifaa Al-Mansour
> *The Lunchbox* directed by Ritesh Batra

P. Kaldas, *Writing the Multicultural Experience*,
https://doi.org/10.1007/978-3-031-06124-0_11

"The Bridge Poem" by Donna Kate Rushin in *This Bridge Called My Back: Writings by Radical Women of Color*, edited by Cherrie Moraga and Gloria Anzaldúa

While *Wadjda* places the daughter as the main character, it is her mother who actually changes throughout the film. After giving birth to Wadjda, she cannot have other children. Her husband is expected to have a male heir and is being pressured to take a second wife. His first wife attempts to hold on to his affection by highlighting her physical beauty and cooking the food he likes; however, she has little power to keep him from taking on a second wife. Her position as a woman unable to provide a son in a society that values the male heir presents an insurmountable obstacle. This movie can create discussion about the types of restrictions placed on women as a result of the power structures embedded in a society.

Throughout *The Lunchbox*, we see Ila in her apartment. That space serves as a physical limitation symbolic of her housewife duties that rarely require her to leave her home. However, her restrictions are more emotional than physical. Her husband, whose face we never fully see, is having an affair and has lost his affection for her. Like Wadjda's mother, she also tries to regain her husband's love by improving her physical appearance and cooking the food he likes. His lack of response imprisons her further into the enclosed space of her apartment and a loveless marriage. This movie can inspire a conversation about how gender roles create limitations.

"The Bridge Poem" by Kate Rushin begins with the anger of serving as the translator for everyone: "I'm sick of seeing and touching/Both sides of things/Sick of being the damn bridge for everybody" (xxi). Being positioned as the explainer forces her to be in service to others who are unable to talk and understand each other without her. This poem can allow us to explore how the expectations that others place on us can force us to play certain roles that restrict us.

Write About an Act of Resistance

While it is important to recognize and investigate the obstacles in our lives, it is equally important to look at our acts of resistance. There is danger in being seen only through the lens of oppression. This happens on a global level when the West views women from certain countries as being oppressed and uses that view to justify political intervention. Women and people of color have always resisted oppression. These individual and collective actions of resistance have changed the course of history. How do we resist the obstacles/limitations/restrictions that affect our lives? How do we find ways to overcome them?

It is important to recognize that acts of resistance are not always clearly visible. They are often private and can manifest in small ways. In Egypt, I met a woman who took literacy classes, so she could learn to sign her own name. Resistance might involve speaking up and can also be expressed in a silence that refuses to give power to the speaker's words. These quieter ways of resistance deserve to be acknowledged.

Prompt: Think of the ways that you express resistance in your life. Consider both the small and large ways you might do this. Create a situation where we see a character resisting an act of oppression. Look deeply to see how less visible actions can be seen as moments of resistance.

Readings: These are the same readings used for the limitations prompt, inviting another look at these texts to discuss how the characters express resistance against social values, find ways to escape from restrictive situations, and use their voices to express resistance.

Wadjda directed by Haifaa Al-Mansour
The Lunchbox directed by Ritesh Batra
"The Bridge Poem" by Donna Kate Rushin in *This Bridge Called My Back: Writings by Radical Women of Color*, edited by Cherrie Moraga and Gloria Anzaldúa

While we can see how Wadjda's desire and persistence in getting a bicycle is an act of resistance against a society that attempts to limit her movements in both physical and metaphorical ways, it is important to recognize the mother's resistance as well. Wadjda's mother can ultimately do nothing about her husband succumbing to pressure and taking another wife. She watches the wedding from the balcony of her own home, unable to participate in an event that affects her life. However, she takes action in another way. After consistently telling Wadjda that she cannot have a bicycle, she purchases the bicycle for her and offers it to her as a symbol of her desire that she will have a different life. The money she uses to purchase the bike is presumably the money she saved to purchase a dress to show off her beauty, so other women would stay away from her husband. This transaction of a dress that attempts to maintain tradition for a bike that challenges tradition expresses her resistance against the limitations imposed on her. This movie can enable us to consider the more subtle ways that resistance takes place.

In *The Lunchbox*, Ila appears locked into her domestic life, maintaining a home for a man who no longer loves her. The letters she shares with the unknown man who receives the lunches she makes gives her an outlet for her thoughts as he responds to her and she feels heard. Her final decision to leave and take her daughter with her is an extraordinary act of liberation, a belief that she deserves happiness rather than a life of servitude that will lead her to replicate her mother's unhappiness. At the end of the movie, we know that she is going to Bhutan, the happiest place in the world. This movie invites us to explore the influences that motivate us to resist and move beyond our circumstances.

In the second half of "The Bridge Poem," the poet rejects the position she has been placed in as translator. She refuses to play the roles people expect of her: "Sick of being your insurance against/The isolation of your self-imposed limitations/Sick of being the crazy at your holiday dinners/Sick of being the odd one at your Sunday Brunches/Sick of being the sole Black friend to 34 individual white people" (xxii). She resists the way others have used her and instead claims her right to be a bridge only to herself: "I must be the bridge to/nowhere/But my true self." Thus, she takes her power back for herself. This poem can bring up ideas about how we can resist the expectations others place on us.

Write About an Object You've Held Onto

As we move from one location to another, items get lost. The things we hold on to can be a way of resisting—a resistance against loss of memory and a way of holding onto identity. Objects carry within them the meaning we give them. And that meaning becomes almost like a talisman against the things that hurt us. Objects become particularly important when there is a history of losing culture or leaving a homeland, where there is a sense of displacement that makes it difficult to feel grounded in our location in the world.

When my parents applied for immigration, they applied to both Canada and the U.S. The man who interviewed us for Canada gave me a pin of the Canadian flag. That was over fifty years ago, and I still have it. Over the years, its meaning has grown larger to encompass the memory of my parents' desire for a better life and their bravery in seeking that life. It holds the possibility of their dreams at that moment, and it holds everything that was lost and gained as a result of that immigration. It also keeps the memory of myself as an eight-year-old child whose life was about to change in ways that were impossible for me to imagine at the time.

Prompt: Make a list of objects that you have held onto for a long time. Jot down a few notes about each one and then select one that you want to explore. Consider when you acquired the object, how you got it, what it meant when you acquired it, and what it means now. What memories/people/locations does it call up for you? How does it matter in your life today?

Readings: These readings can lead to discussions about objects that carry family history, that connect us to other people, and that are passed on through the generations.

> *The Namesake* by Jhumpa Lahiri
> *Everything I Never Told You* by Celeste Ng
> *Homegoing* by Yaa Gyasi

In *The Namesake*, the book that saves Ashoke's life remains significant even after it is lost in the train crash. He names his son after the author, keeping the memory of the book alive. On his son's fourteenth birthday, Ashoke gives his son a copy of the book. Gogol is uninterested, so the book remains on his bookcase unread. In one of the final scenes of the novel, Gogol pulls the book off the shelf, "And then another book, never read, long forgotten, catches his eye … he opens it to the title page. … 'For Gogol Ganguli … The man who gave you his name, from the man who gave you your name.' … The name he had so detested, here hidden and preserved—that was the first thing his father had given him" (288–289). Finding the book again marks that moment of acceptance for Gogol, of who he is, his name, and everything his father has given him. This aspect of the novel can create discussion about an object given as a gift and the meaning it carries.

In *Everything I Never Told You*, the only thing that Marilyn retrieves from her mother's home after her mother dies is her cookbook. The cookbook with her mother's notes is emblematic of her mother's identity and her beliefs about gender roles. For Marilyn, it represents everything she does not want to be, everything she has tried to resist and failed. After Marilyn leaves her family, her daughter Lydia hides the cookbook, believing it is what caused her mother's sadness and her departure from the family. As Marilyn scours Lydia's room for answers after Lydia's death, she finally finds the cookbook: "Somehow Lydia had known: that this book had pulled on her mother like a heavy, heavy stone. … She had hidden it, all those years; she had piled book after book atop it, weighting it down, so her mother would never have to see it again" (247). It is at that moment through the cookbook that Marilyn begins to understand her own daughter and how she chose obedience to please her. This novel raises issues about the objects that haunt us and reflect the burdens we carry.

In *Homegoing*, the first woman, Maame, passes on a necklace to each of her daughters. One is lost in the dungeon of Cape Coast Castle, and the other is passed on through the generations. Each time the necklace is given to someone, it is attached to the story of the family, and history is passed on with it. When James passes the necklace to his daughter, Abena, he says, "'This belonged to my grandmother, your great-grandmother Effia. It was given to her by her own mother.' 'Effia,' Abena repeated. It was the first time she had heard the name of one of her ancestors, and she savored the taste of the name on her tongue" (152). In this way, the necklace becomes an object of remembrance. When the descendants of both sides of the family meet and the necklace is exchanged, a full circle of family unity is achieved, healing the fracture that took place when the two sisters were separated, one sold into slavery and the other remaining in Ghana. The necklace that remains lost in the dungeon exists as a call to return home for the descendants of Esi and the generations forced into slavery. This aspect of the novel can generate a discussion about items that are passed on through the generations and the stories they carry with them as well as those items that are lost.

Write About a Secret

Secrets exist in everyone's life. For those who come from a multicultural background, those secrets are often embedded in our culture, which determines what we can speak about publicly and what is expected to remain hidden within the family. Such secrets are often connected to cultural values. Speaking those secrets aloud becomes an act of defiance, a way to break through cultural taboos. It can also cause breaks in family structure and destroy a precarious system. Sometimes, revealing secrets can lead to healing relationships, trauma, and offer a better way to move forward.

I grew up hearing many family secrets—an uncle who could not marry the woman he loved, an aunt whose child died under mysterious circumstances, and a child who ran away from home. Carrying these secrets with their incomplete stories led me to writing fiction, so that I could reveal the secrets and complete the stories within the fabric of imagination. It allowed me to unearth those secrets and look at them more closely.

Prompt: Think of the secrets that exist within your family. Consider the ones where you know the full story and the ones where you might only know a small part. What lies beneath these secrets? What values and beliefs make these stories that cannot be told? Why are these things that must be hidden?

What might happen if they are revealed? Write from these questions, exploring them through any genre to break through the cultural taboos.

Readings: These readings can lead to discussions about what we do with the secrets passed on to us, how secrets create a cycle of abuse, and how revealing secrets leads to healing.

> *The Woman Warrior* by Maxing Hong Kingston
> *Purple Hibiscus* by Chimamanda Ngozi Adichie
> *Arabian Jazz* by Diana Abu Jaber

The Woman Warrior begins with the mother saying, "You must not tell anyone" (3). It is this secret passed on to Kingston from her mother that propels the book forward. As Kingston tries to make up for the missing pieces of this story, she creates her own scenarios of how her aunt might have gotten pregnant and how the story unfolded. In one scenario, she imagines that her aunt was forced into a relationship, and in another, she imagines that her aunt sought out the relationship, each time filling in the details of the secret she has been told. Kingston knows the power of revealing her aunt's secret, ending by saying that "The real punishment was not the raid swiftly inflicted by the villagers, but the family's deliberately forgetting her" (16). She has broken this punishment by speaking of her aunt, thus revealing the secret becomes an act of resistance against that tradition. This book invites readers to share the secrets that have been passed on to them and consider how carrying these secrets affects their lives.

In *Purple Hibiscus*, Kambili carries the secret of her father's abuse toward her mother, her brother, and herself. She upholds her father's powerful reputation in the community by keeping this secret and acting obediently to him. This secret creates a disjunction between the family's public image and their private life. The novel is filled with references to Kambili's inability to speak, remaining silent or stuttering when she attempts to talk. When she meets her cousin, she says, "I wondered how Amaka did it, how she opened her mouth and had words flow easily out" (99). When the abuse goes too far and she reveals the secret to others around her, she is finally released from that bond of obedience and able to help her family begin the journey of recovery. This book can initiate discussion about the secret abuses that take place within families and also the public images that families and individuals create to hide their private lives.

In *Arabian Jazz*, Fatima holds the secret that comes from the memory of her younger sisters who were buried when they were infants, presumably because her parents could not afford to take care of any more children. "Fatima recalled assisting in two, possibly three other furtive burials. ... The memories moved in and out of her" (119). These memories hold Fatima captive to the past, and she is unable to share them with anyone, carrying the burden by herself. They haunt her and keep her from expressing emotion to those around her, appearing to be almost a caricature character. It is only when she releases the secret and speaks it aloud that she finds a release from the past. The healing begins there and continues when she learns that her sisters back in Jordan have also figured out the truth and have found a way to commemorate the death of those siblings. "We laid the babies to rest. ... Nothing to do know but mourn and reflect. We want her to come back, to visit and see her home and family again. To know that it's over" (354). This book enables us to consider the secrets that we keep to ourselves, especially those based on vague memories, and how they affect us.

Write About Movement

Having a multicultural identity means that you are in constant movement. That movement may be physical or metaphorical. As we move from one country to another, from one community to another, from one neighborhood to another, we need to consider how we traverse those spaces. As we walk on the street, ride a bus, train, or plane, how do we negotiate these spaces that are in between and how do we carry our bodies from one location to the other? Do we walk differently? Do we dress differently? How do we negotiate space and identity as we move through the world?

When I return to Egypt, I walk differently. I hold my body closer, move my arms less, and my stride shortens. I intuitively mimic the walk of other women around me. I am more aware of the space I take up in a crowded city and also more aware of the male gaze that follows women on the street. In the U.S., where space is more abundant, I lengthen my stride and I walk with more confidence, which can protect me from the male gaze.

Prompt: Think about how you move through different spaces. Do you walk differently depending on your location? How do you negotiate being on a bus, a train, a plane? What happens as you are moving? Do you attract the attention of others? How comfortable do you feel in your body? How do you feel about moving through the space—do you feel a sense of ownership and freedom or a sense of crowdedness and enclosure?

Readings: These readings can lead to discussions about the restrictions placed on our movement, the way we transform ourselves as we move from one location to another, and the way we take ownership of our movements.

Wadjda directed by Haifaa Al-Mansour
New Kid by Jerry Craft
"Escape from the Dysphesiac People" by Brandon Hobson in *The Best American Short Stories, 2021*

Wadjda is the first feature film made by a female Saudi Arabian director. The movie can be seen as an exploration of movement. Wadjda lives in Saudi Arabia and longs to have a bicycle, so she can race her best friend, Abdullah. But girls are not allowed to ride bicycles. In many of the scenes, we see Wadjda walking or running in the streets while dressed in the abbaya that inhibits her movement, but the sneakers she insists on wearing despite school regulations allow her to move faster. Her perseverance and the change in her mother's life finally enable her to have a bicycle, and we see how she enters the world with greater mobility, the bicycle becoming a metaphor for her ability to create her own life. This movie can help us to explore the things that increase our movements like our shoes, clothing, or transportation.

In one of the notebook sketches in *New Kid*, Jerry Craft depicts himself taking the train from his neighborhood to his private school. As he passes each station, he transforms his appearance and manner according to the area he is in and the types of people on the train. He keeps his hoodie on to appear tough or takes it off to appear less threatening. He does math problems to appear smart, so others will not be threatened by him. While he remains in the same spot on the train during the entire journey, he changes to suit the neighborhood through which he is traveling and the people who occupy the train. As he says, "Fitting in on the ride to school is hard work! I have to be like a chameleon" (56). This is more than adaptation. It is an act of survival in potentially hostile environments. This segment can initiate discussion about how we change ourselves as we move from place to place.

The narrator of "Escape from the Dysphesiac People" describes how he is forcibly taken from his home and moved by train and car to a place devoid of life. "We drove through winding streets lined with barren trees, past a tall grain elevator and empty buildings. There were deserted motels with shattered windows and broken signs. Empty parking lots, trash strewn on the streets" (55). He is taken to a ranch where he is told to work with other Indians with little food. The apparitions of his ancestors make him realize that he has to leave, and when he has the chance, he runs. "I ran. I ran from the barn as hard as I could" (61). He uses his own body to create the movement that finally allows him to escape and return home. This story can generate conversation about the movements forced upon us and those we choose for ourselves.

Write in Multiple Languages

For those of us who live inside more than one language, we must consider how to express that on the literary page. Bringing another language into our writing is a way of claiming an experience that can only be articulated outside of English. Creating a text that uses another language along with English in a country that has tried to make English the official language, has undermined those who do not speak English, and has penalized those who speak it with an accent is an act of resistance against the notion of a dominant language and the attempt to erase other languages. In many countries, students learn a second and a third language by the time they graduate from high school. Here, our language requirements are minimal, and few people know a second language. Yet, we expect those who immigrate to America to learn English quickly and fluently. And we place the children of those immigrants in remedial classes and treat them as if they are less intelligent. As a nation, we fall behind in our ability to recognize the value of other languages. This history goes at least as far back as punishing Native students when they spoke their own language at the boarding schools. Other languages have often been viewed as threatening to the attempt to create a homogenous nation.

I recall one student who came into my class upset, because in another class, she was reprimanded for using Spanish in one of her poems and told that she must write only in English. It was not the first time I had heard something like this. The negative response to the use of other languages often comes from fear and the arrogance of believing you have a right to have access to everything, that the writer must explain it to you. For this student, bringing Spanish into her poem was a way of articulating her lived experience. Language is a place where we live, and this student lived inside both English and Spanish. For the reader, it was an invitation to enter into a space where they could engage with what it means to not understand.

Prompt: Bring another language into a piece of writing. Even if you don't know your native language fluently, there are words that are probably familiar to you, especially those words that cannot be so easily translated. Consider how two languages can weave together, either by a seamless blend or perhaps by emphasizing the distinction between the two languages. How can two languages speak to one another on the page and how can they tell a story that goes beyond a singular experience?

Readings: These readings can lead to discussions about how certain languages have been viewed as threatening, how meaning cannot be easily translated, and how two languages can be used in a single work.

Sweet Land by Ali Selim

"How to Tame a Wild Tongue" in *Borderlands/La Frontera: The New Mestiza* by
Gloria Anzaldúa

"Cairo Walk" in *Egyptian Compass* by Pauline Kaldas

Sweet Land focuses on a German woman who arrives in Minnesota shortly
after WWI to marry a Norwegian man who lives in a small farming community. The community is suspicious of her because she is German, and the
couple have difficulty finding a way to get married. Several times in the movie,
she is told to speak English only, "no German here." The first instance occurs
in the church when they are about to be married. The priest stops her and
refuses to marry them. Her language is an indication of her threatening identity. Before WWI, German was a widely taught language in the U.S. With
WWI, laws were enacted to prohibit the teaching of German as it came to be
seen as a threat. Looking at those moments in the movie when German is
used reveals the way that language, identity, and politics collapse into one
another. This movie can initiate conversation about how language has been
viewed as a threat. This has been especially true of Arabic where people reading Arabic books on planes have been reported for seeming dangerous.
Interestingly, *Sweet Land* was written and directed by Ali Selim who is
Egyptian and German.

In "How to Tame a Wild Tongue," Anzaldúa speaks about Chicano identity with a focus on language. She recalls the attempt to take her language
away, "I remember being caught speaking Spanish at recess—that was good
for three licks on the knuckles with a sharp ruler" (53). She makes the point
that language and identity are inextricably linked and to take away a language
is to take away a people's culture: "Chicano Spanish sprang out of the
Chicanos' need to identify ourselves as a distinct people" (55). The essay is
bilingual, written in Spanish and English, exemplifying the Chicano experience. Anzaldúa explains the importance of this by saying, "Until I am free to
write bilingually and to switch codes without having always to translate, while
I still have to speak English or Spanish when I would rather speak Spanglish,
and as long as I have to accommodate the English speakers rather than having
them accommodate me, my tone will be illegitimate" (59). In this essay, she
does precisely this, bringing Spanish into her writing without translation in
order to express her full identity. This piece can raise issues about the political
aspects of language and how new languages are created to reflect a specific
identity.

My poem, "Cairo Walk," is an attempt to relay the types of comments that
men make to women on the streets of Cairo. A simple translation did not

capture the meaning or the rhythm of those comments. While transliteration helped to express the sounds, it still felt insufficient. Once I added the comments in Arabic script, the poem felt complete, allowing me to let these words be expressed in a layered pattern on the page: "asel [written in Arabic script]/'asel'/(honey)" (60). When I read this poem at the American University in Cairo, I read the lines in Arabic, and half the audience laughed. Then I read their translation, and the other half of the audience laughed. In this way, I could reach a wider audience, and the poem could speak in two languages simultaneously. This poem can open up a discussion on how to use multiple languages in a piece of writing and the effect this can have on the reader.

Self-Designed Assignment

This is an opportunity to draw on everything you have done and develop your own project. You can write a completely new piece, you can expand a previous assignment, or you can combine several things you wrote to create a single work. You can also use this opportunity to envision a cohesive project that might lead to a book-length manuscript. This could be composed of a single narrative or shorter interrelated pieces. Creating a longer manuscript opens up the opportunity to give attention to the shape and structure of the entire work.

Approaches

Write from Anger

Anger is an emotion that has often been denied to people of color. Our anger at racism has led to stereotypes such as the angry Black man/woman, the spicy Latina, and the violent Arab. When we express anger at discrimination, we are often labeled as "emotional," which becomes a way of dismissing the content of our anger and the issues we want to make visible. Thinking about anger is essential for those of us who write from outside the margins of society. We need to consider what angers us, how we have chosen to express/not express that anger, and how our anger has been received by others. Many of us learn to keep our anger tucked in so as not to be labeled emotional, confrontational, or to avoid serious repercussions.

© The Author(s), under exclusive license to Springer Nature Switzerland AG 2022
P. Kaldas, *Writing the Multicultural Experience*,
https://doi.org/10.1007/978-3-031-06124-0_12

Writing from a place of anger can be a way to advocate for change. Owning our anger as a force of power is necessary for our survival. Given where we are as a society, it is important to also consider the power of collective anger as we have seen when protests have risen against police violence. Our anger is both individual and collective, and acknowledging it can be a source of empowerment and a move toward change.

Prompt: These poems express anger, but none of them use curse words to do so. While such words can be powerful, they can also weaken meaning because of their overuse. Writing out of anger without using such language pushes us to articulate the specificity of that anger. It challenges us to identify it and explore it like these poets who delve into the history and politics that result in the acts that cause their anger. This prompt asks you to write out of anger with attention to language.

Readings: These readings address the power of anger to effect change, to reveal the truth, and to resist oppression.

"Power" in *The Collected Poems of Audre Lorde* by Audre Lorde
"Today Was a Bad Day Like TB" in *Not Vanishing* by Chrystos
"Exotic" in *Born Palestinian, Born Black* by Suheir Hammad

Audre Lorde's poem, "Power," emerges out of the actual story of a white policeman being acquitted for shooting and killing a Black ten-year-old boy. The poem explores the anger of the speaker and the way that bottled up anger against racism can fester and then explode in destructive ways: "my power too will run corrupt as poisonous mold/or lie limp and useless as an unconnected wire" (320). While this poem was written in 1978, it could have easily been written today in response to police brutality. It is an exploration of the violence experienced by Black people, the loss of power, and the consequences of suppressed anger. For more about Lorde, the movie, *A Litany for Survival: The Life and Work of Audre Lorde*, is an excellent one to watch.

Chrystos is a Native American poet whose work does not shy away from anger. In "Today Was a Bad Day Like TB," the anger is directed against the co-opting of Native American culture—whether through museum exhibits of objects to which whites claim ownership or the use of Native designs to sell goods without permission or compensation. It is an indictment of the way white culture turns other cultures into commodities that can be bought, sold, and exhibited. "Today was a day I wanted to beat up the smirking man wearing/a pack with a Haida design from Moe's bookstore/Listen Moe's How many Indians do you have working there?/How much money are you sending the Haida people/to use their sacred raven design?" (61). Chrystos's anger culminates in the image of spitting up like TB, a disease that whites brought with them through colonization and that infected Native peoples. "Today was a day like TB/you cough & cough trying to get it out/all that comes/is blood & spit" (61). The power of this poem lies precisely in the anger of its response to this theft of Native culture. It becomes a reclamation of culture and the history of destruction that Native peoples have suffered.

Suheir Hammad is a Palestinian American poet who grew up in Brooklyn. It is easy to find clips of her reading "Exotic" on YouTube, and it is worth hearing her read it live to see how the form on the page transfers to the spoken word. This poem focuses on the exoticizing of women of color. Here, Hammad rejects how she is perceived by men who exoticize her, claiming her ordinariness, particularly in the line "the beat of my lashes against each other/ain't some dark desert beat/it's just a blink/get over it" (69). The poem opens up toward the end as she lists the stereotypes that have been applied to women of different cultures, revealing that this experience affects all women of color. It is a powerful poem that expresses anger through rejection of the objectification of women and reclaims the self.

Write from Imagination

Many of us are second, third, or subsequent generations of immigrants. We have some knowledge of our family history, but we may or may not have visited our native country, and our cultural knowledge may have been diluted through the generations. As a result, we might be reluctant to write out of our culture because of this lack of knowledge. Finding a way to claim our story can be challenging. One way to address this is through the opening of imagination. How do you fill in what you do not know? How do you claim the stories to which you do not have complete access? Making a leap into imagination gives you permission to tell your story however incomplete it may be. Using our imagination creates an opening for storytelling that exists somewhere between truth and fiction. Our ability to imagine is a powerful tool, a way to understand what we do not know.

This space between fiction and nonfiction opens possibilities for multicultural writers that deserves to be explored. For a long time, I felt frustrated by the small pieces of stories I was told about my family history. These fragments served as a beginning for my fiction, where I had to step into that place of imagination in order to discover the story.

Prompt: Begin with a story that exists only as a fragment. Write what you know then take the leap to imagine the rest of the story. Take that avenue of fiction to seek out a truth. Allow your imagination to wander. Paint the story with details—focus in on scenes, dialogue, setting, tensions. Bring the characters to life through your imagination.

Readings: These readings offer examples of how to use imagination to make sense of the stories we are told, how to bring life to the stories we hear, and how to resist the silence of certain stories.

> *The Woman Warrior* by Maxine Hong Kingston
> "These Words" in *Geographies of Light* by Lisa Suhair Majaj
> "Emmet Till's Name Still Catches in My Throat" by Marilyn Nelson in *Resisting Arrest: Poems to Stretch the Sky*, edited by Tony Medina

The Woman Warrior is an ideal book to show the power of imagination in writing. Beginning with the fragment she is told of her aunt's pregnancy and suicide, Kingston immediately claims what is missing. She goes on to describe two different scenarios for her aunt. Each of these stories begin with words like "perhaps," indicating to the reader that this is an imagined scenario. This simple technique opens a space where the reader can join the author in imagining other possible stories for her aunt. This method continues throughout the novel. In the second section, Kingston takes the myth of Fa Mu Lan and transforms it. In response to the negative critiques she received for changing the traditional legend, Kingston says in an interview with Arturo Islas and Marilyn Yalom that "[m]yth is vibrant and alive as long as it keeps changing. When people emigrate from China (or from anywhere), they bring myths with them, but they change the myths. And if they don't change those myths, those myths are useless and die" (40). This can apply to those who are second and third generation immigrants, who must not only investigate their past but must also create their future, not by repeating what has come before them but by making something new from the past. One of the strongest acts of imagination in Kingston's book comes in the way she tells Moon Orchid's story. After Kingston tells us the story in its entirety, she reveals that she was not actually present at any of these events. "In fact, it wasn't me my brother told about going to Los Angeles; one of my sisters told me what he'd told her. His version of the story may be better than mine because of its bareness, not twisted into designs" (163). In her design, Kingston creates the details and the emotions of the story for herself. This process of imagining what is missing culminates at the end of the novel when she tells a story where the first part comes from her mother and the second part from her. This act of braiding fragments and adding imagination to create a meaningful story is an essential part of how we become writers.

"These Words" is a poem written in response to the true story of Rana, a young woman in Palestine who was turned away at a checkpoint when she tried to get to the hospital to give birth. As a result, both she and her child died. Majaj imagines the young woman and the thoughts in her mind: "Did she hum quietly/to the child in her belly,/tremble when artillery pounded/the streets, when planes rained fire—/cries shaking the air" (98). That act of imagination brings Rana to life, allowing the reader to enter into her experience and her fear. This poem offers an example of taking a real event and adding imagination to bring it to life.

In "Emmet Till's Name Still Catches in My Throat," Nelson uses imagination to tell the story of Emmet Till through details that create his humanity. "In his suitcase/she'd packed dungarees, T-shirts, underwear,/and comic books. She'd given him a note/for the conductor, waved to his chubby face,/ wondered if he'd remember to brush his hair" (68). In presenting these details through the mother's perspective, going as far as entering her thoughts, she brings Emmet Till to life as the child that he was. Her act of imagination becomes an act of resistance against the dehumanization and brutality that Emmet Till experienced.

Write from Humor

The ability to look at life's experiences through the lens of humor offers a new perspective. It can be a way to talk about difficult subjects, allowing readers to engage with topics that they might otherwise resist. It can also be a source of empowerment. Living as a minority within the U.S. is filled with harsh moments. Telling our stories through the avenue of humor allows us to take ownership of those stories. By turning what is thrown at us and transforming it into the shape of humor, we diffuse it and take back the power. Humor does not have to be the laugh out loud kind. It can be a story with a light touch or the kind of humor that causes a slight smile. The ability to showcase the difficult with the humorous can open a new path into storytelling.

An excellent essay about how to bring humor into your writing is "The Comfortable Chair: Using Humor in Creative Nonfiction" by Dinty Moore. This essay offers advice regarding the techniques of humor, such as exaggeration, juxtaposition, irony, and satire that make humor most effective. Two particularly helpful points are "to avoid seeming to look down at the subjects of your writing" and to remember that "the humor takes a backseat to the story being told." Moore also explains that you cannot force humor; rather,

"You have to be amused yourself, and you have to take honest pleasure in your amusement" (128).

Prompt: Think of an event that you would normally view through a serious lens. Consider how you might look at it through humor. Turn that lens of humor onto yourself. Pay attention to your quirks and idiosyncrasies and don't be afraid to put them on the page. Approach the story from a more light-hearted way and see where it takes you.

Readings: These readings show how humor can reveal more serious concerns, how it can diffuse a tense situation, and how it can allow us to see the humorous side of our experiences.

> "Save Me, Mickey" in *Funny in Farsi* by Firoozeh Dumas
> *Sharon and My Mother-in-Law* by Suad Amiry
> "How to plan an Arab-American Wedding that will please everyone (except you)" by Susan Muaddi Darraj in *Middle East Eye*

In the essays that make up *Funny in Farsi*, Dumas enters her stories dealing with politics, language, and cultural differences as an Iranian American through humor. She allows us to laugh while also revealing the hardships that she and her family experienced. In "Save Me, Mickey," she tells the story of getting lost in Disneyland. At the office where she is taken, there is a young boy who has also lost his family and does not speak English. The woman in charge asks Dumas to speak to him, and despite Dumas's explanation that they do not speak the same language, the woman insists until Dumas complies to put a stop to the woman's request. "I walked up to the boy … and said in Persian, 'Are you Iranian?' The boy stopped crying for a moment, then let out the loudest scream heard since biblical times. Not only was he separated from his loved ones, he was now trapped in the Tower of Babel" (21). While we can see the humor in this scene, we can also see how the ignorance of language and culture can be damaging to children. It is possible to focus on any essay and explore how Dumas uses humor and how that humor unveils the serious side of the subject.

The Palestinian crisis is a topic that does not readily appear to be conducive to humor, and yet, Amiry manages to approach it in that way in her memoir, *Sharon and My Mother-in-Law*. Through humor, she pushes the reader to see deeper into the subject. In one scene, Amiry is trying to get her mother-in-law to pack her things and leave her home, which is in a dangerous area, so she can come stay with them. As she watches her mother-in-law debating which dress to take, the scene opens the curtain of humor with the mother-in-law asking questions such as "Shall I bring my purple dress? … Do you think yellow goes with purple? ... Shall I take winter or summer clothes" (147–148). When Amiry tells her to leave her things and they can come back to get them later, her mother-in-law responds, "That's what we said in 1948 when we left our house in Jaffa" (149). The reminder that a temporary departure sometimes becomes permanent places the humor in a different context, allowing the reader to see what is actually at stake in this scene.

The title of the essay, "How to plan an Arab-American wedding that will please everyone (except you)" sets the humorous tone of the essay. Darraj establishes the goal of an Arab American wedding when she says, "But realise it's not actually your wedding." Rather, the wedding centers on making sure that everyone else enjoys themselves, especially the "Aunties" who represent the entire extended Arab family. The author captures this moment perfectly when she describes one Aunt sitting on her balcony in her village and pulling out her iPhone to watch the wedding video. Darraj shifts the way we think about weddings to create the humor. She goes through a list of things, such as the venue, the seating plan, the band, and the food, explaining how to make decisions based on the guests rather than on what the bride or groom want. For the guest list, she explains, "Sure, you have 64 first cousins, but the Arab quota system requires you ask one cousin from each family to participate. So, accept that you'll have 14 bridesmaids. Maybe three flower girls. That your photographer will have to arrange everyone like a football team and use the wide lens." This essay takes a stressful event and turns it around to see it through the lens of humor, allowing readers, especially those who are Arab American to enjoy viewing their cultural practices in a light-hearted way while also showing the value of the communal nature of this cultural practice.

Experimentations/Innovation

Craft is often highlighted in creative writing classrooms; however, focusing too much on craft can negate significant concerns of writers of color. As Lee says in the Introduction to her book, *How Dare We! Write*, "For writers of color, writing isn't just about process and craft, but also the challenges we face as writers, and how we overcome those challenges" (ii). Chavez quotes her husband, explaining his view that "a blind fixation on craft 'is a cover for avoiding issues of marginalization and politics of narrative'" (qtd. in Chavez 122).

Innovation and improvisation have been an integral part of the work of diverse artists. The way we tell a story is revealed in the way we put our vision on the page. Traditional Western novels lean toward a linear structure with a clear main character. This form can be inadequate for telling the stories of people of color. Our lives do not always fit into a linear pattern, and our sense of self is often intricately connected to our communities. Mura explains that his writing emerged out of acknowledging the inadequacy of what was available to him, saying that "the tools the culture had given me to express my identity and experience were inadequate, that they carried with them limitations imposed by history, politics, and culture" (12). Circular patterns, fragmented patterns, and communal perspectives often mark the work of writers of color. After taking my course on Multicultural Women Writers, one of my students remarked in her final reflection paper that "a lot of these stories were like Russian nesting dolls in that they contained stories within stories within stories."

My life began in Egypt and then moved to the U.S., but if I wrote my story in this way, it would be incomplete. I returned to Egypt five times, two of those times for longer periods. But even without the geographical movement, my life in the U.S. contains memories of being in Egypt and a connection to my family who is still there. Such life experiences require new forms of storytelling. As a young reader, I was always perplexed by the American stories I read where the focus was clearly pointed on the main character—I often wondered, where are the parents, the aunts and uncles and cousins, and the watchful community? I had learned to see my identity and my actions from a communal lens, but the stories I read did not reflect that experience.

An awareness of these issues affects how we approach narrative perspective—do we want a single narrator, a communal narrator, or multiple narrators? It can also affect the notion of a main character—the Horatio Alger model of one person triumphing over adversity is not one that often fits our lives. Can there be multiple main characters? Can the main character be a community? With each of the prompts in this book, think about how you might experiment to enhance the piece you are writing. Here are some possibilities.

Form/Structure

Mosaic—This method allows intense focus on a single moment then combines those moments to tell the story. It works well to highlight singular events and opens room for connections to emerge in unexpected ways. This form works well for travel pieces, and it can also work well for a memory piece as our memories are often fragments of experience that stay with us. The use of parts to create a whole also invites a different way of reading, where the reader becomes more actively engaged in the reading process as they consider how the fragments of the mosaic relate to one another. These fragments can be separated by white space, asterisks, or subtitles. There are various ways to approach the form of the mosaic to create a narrative. Consider an experience you've had and write about specific moments of that experience to create a mosaic piece. For an excellent essay on this form, see Brenda Miller's essay, "A Braided Heart: Shaping the Lyric Essay" in *Creative Nonfiction*.

Genre—Writing about the same experience in multiple genres can create different emphasis. The poem can serve as a spotlight while the essay can enlarge the canvas, and the short story can extend further with its fictional leap. Experiment by writing a poem about an experience, then a personal essay, then a story about the same experience. For an excellent essay by a writer who has written in all three genres, see Judith Ortiz Cofer's "But Tell it Slant: From Poetry to Prose and Back Again" in *Creative Nonfiction*.

Linear/Circular—The chronological structure is often our default—we start at the beginning and we finish at the end. However, such clear movement is not always the best method for telling a story. Consider where the story might begin—perhaps in the middle at the most pivotal moment, perhaps at the end and then it can make its way back to show the pattern of events, or perhaps it can move back and forth from the present to the past. Try beginning with the most pivotal moment of the story then work around it to reveal how that moment occurred, or begin at the end and work back to the beginning. For examples, see *Purple Hibiscus* by Chimamanda Ngozi Adichie, *Everything I Never Told You* by Celeste Ng, and *Catfish and Mandala* by Andrew X. Pham.

Narrative Perspective

In fiction, we have several choices for narrative perspective, including first person, third person limited, second person, and omniscient. When we write creative nonfiction, the assumption is that we will use first person to tell our story. It is an approach that works well. However, delving into difficult material through a first-person perspective can become emotionally taxing to a point where the writing does not happen. I had one student who was having difficulty writing about some of her life experiences, often skimming the surface. When I suggested she write from a third-person perspective, her writing opened up, and she was able to move beyond the surface. Writing in third person can offer an alternative that allows us to enter the material from enough distance to explore it. The distancing of self is also perhaps more than a shift in narrative perspective. For many diverse writers, life is lived in multiple identities. We often act as translators of culture; therefore, we exist both inside and outside of our experiences. Writing about ourselves from a third-person perspective is another way to see ourselves in the world. Playing with narrative perspective becomes a way of articulating the truth of how we function in our different communities.

A good exercise is to take a scene and write it from different characters' perspective, then from an omniscient perspective then from a plural perspective. Many novels have been written with chapters switching from one character's perspective to another such as *Madam Fate* by Marcia Douglas, *Homegoing* by Yaa Gyasi, *The Book of Unknown Americans* by Cristina Henríquez, and *Sitt Marie Rose* by Etel Adnan. The key here is to recognize and experiment with various options rather than assuming there is only one way to tell a story.

Main Characters

I recall the first book that made me think differently about the notion of a main character. It was *God's Bits of Wood* by Sembene Ousmane, which I read in an African Literature class at Binghamton University. The novel focuses on the Railway worker's strike that took place in West Africa during the colonial era. As we discussed the novel, it became clear that there was not a single main character. No one individual triumphed. Together, the community faced struggle, overcame obstacles, and survived. The concept of a community as a main character instinctively made sense to me as I considered the interconnectedness within my own culture. The assumption of a single main character gets drilled into us from our early school years. Shifting that idea can be challenging but can allow for the possibility of expressing a more communal vision on the page.

Poetry and Prose

When I began writing, I gravitated toward poetry. At some point, I naturally moved to creative nonfiction. The result is that poetry and prose blended together in my writing. In that space between genres, the two forms found a way to exist simultaneously. "Shifting Paces," which appears in *Letters from Cairo*, was one of the first creative nonfiction pieces I wrote. It moves between prose and poetry, the prose stopping to make space for a few lines of poetry and then moving again to prose that borders on poetry. Some of the prose is written in fragmented phrases, while some is in complete sentences. Given that this piece recalls much of what my husband and I experienced while living in Egypt for three years, it makes sense that it blurs genres as a way to mirror our complex experience of what it meant for me to return to a homeland I had left as a child and what it meant for my African American husband to be in Egypt. I recall another moment when I read my short creative nonfiction piece, "Aunt Helena," at a conference, and afterwards, someone told me how much they enjoyed my poem. This moment of genre fluidity meant that I had succeeded in bringing the lyrical into my prose in such a way that the two genres became indistinguishable.

The study of poetry is essential for all writers as it teaches us the most about language—how each word, each line, each sound matters. We also learn about simile, metaphor, imagery, symbolism. Most importantly, poetry requires the courage and skill of playing with language, manipulating it to see how far we can stretch it to convey meaning in new ways. It also teaches us about form, something that is often neglected in prose. How does the piece look on the page and how does that form contribute to meaning? Consider when a prose piece is all long paragraphs on the page or when it is all dialogue or when a one sentence paragraph appears in the midst of longer paragraphs. Everything we learn from poetry can travel to prose.

There are many ways to bring poetry and prose together. Ortiz Cofer's book, *The Latin Deli*, contains stories, essays, and poems that exist alongside each other. The order of these pieces creates a conversation with each one enhancing the meaning of the others. They are in dialogue with one another. You can also experiment with poetry and prose existing in the same piece, moving from one to the other, either in a fluid way where the genres blend or perhaps with sharper transitions between the genres. You might also attempt the lyric essay, which brings elements of poetry such as symbolism and imagery into a prose piece.

This blending of the genres can open up new avenues of writing for those who choose to write from a multicultural perspective. Given the layers of experience and identity that we bring to our writing, experimenting with the blurring of genres can be a way to express our complex experiences, to discover new ways to tell our stories, and to tell multiple stories simultaneously.

Text and Visual

Many writers and visual artists have brought the textual and the visual together to create works of art that speak beyond a single artistic medium. There is an excitement in bringing an art form outside of writing onto the page. It challenges us to experience the text in a multi-sensory way. As readers, we must enter the text through a double doorway to explore how text and visual interact to create a narrative. All writers would benefit from learning another art form: visual art, acting, filmmaking, photography, dance, music, and so on. Visual art teaches us to see, to really see something. That attention to visual detail invites us to write from a different lens. During my first painting class, I was drawing a palm tree from a photograph. My painted tree didn't look right. I was busy painting the green of the leaves when the instructor came over and told me to look again at the photograph, noting that the leaves were not only green. There was white and purple in them. I looked again and hesitantly attempted to add those colors to my painting. That is when the leaves looked right. Visual art challenges us to see beyond the surface of our daily use of sight, and when we bring that knowledge into literature, it adds another dimension that creates a multifaceted art form.

Graphic books are of course a prime example of the fusion of art and text. We must read both the visual and the words in order to take in the complete work. *The Four Immigrants Manga* is considered one of the first graphic books. The author, Henry (Yoshitaka) Kiyama, wrote and illustrated the book, creating a complete vision of the story he wanted to write. There are other ways to bring these two art forms together. In *Desert Exile*, Yoshiko Uchida's memoir of her family's time in the Japanese concentration camps, she includes several photographs, which is a common practice in family memoirs. By including the photographs, Uchida makes visible this part of American history.

A less obvious way of bringing the visual is through the form of the words on the page. In *Zong*, M. Nourbese Philip places the text fragmented across the page, opening up the white space. In order to read the book, we must engage with it like a painting, looking at it from different angles, getting closer and more distant to see the larger shape and the minute details. Philips demands more of us in this text about the slave ship where the captain ordered that 150 captured Africans be drowned at sea so that the owners of the ship could collect the insurance money. The form is essential to this narrative that cannot be viewed through a linear lens but holds a story that has been manipulated throughout history. Here, Philips creates her own manipulation of text to tell the story fully.

When I was putting together the manuscript of my book, *Letters from Cairo*, I knew that I wanted to include the voices of my family. I had journal excerpts from my husband and emails and poems from my older daughter, but my younger daughter was only five when we were in Egypt. She spent most of her time drawing, and it was through these drawings that she expressed her experiences and observations. She drew a variety of pictures, including one of herself at school, one of the Egyptian Tooth Fairy, and one of our home in Virginia. These pictures where her voice, and I was fortunate to be able to include them in the book, so that her experience could be part of this family memoir.

For those who live in multiple cultures, the visual is often associated with memory. A memory of a home in another place, a memory of relatives you can no longer see, a memory of a landscape. These are a visceral part of our experience. Consider the ways you can bring the visual and the textual together in your work. Experiment with various forms, depending on your abilities and the materials you have. You might begin by gathering together some visual artifacts and writing in response to each of them to see where that takes you.

Reflection: A Writer's Identity

After working through these readings and prompts, it is important to take time to reflect on your own identity as a writer. As you review the following readings, consider how these writers speak about where they position themselves and how they claim a chosen rather than an imposed writing identity. Using the readings as takeoff points, think about how you define yourself as a writer—the answer might be singular or multiple. What do you see as your community of writers? How do you position yourself among other communities? These questions are not meant to lead to a static answer—our identities and communities remain fluid and transformative.

I began by thinking of myself as an Egyptian American writer. My political awareness led me to embrace the term Arab American and to position myself within that community. As my reading expanded, I also recognized that I was an immigrant writer, placing myself in a wider context. I have been defined as an Arab writer, an African writer, and a Southern writer, among others. Each of these identities adds another concentric circle to my sense of where I belong. I have learned to embrace them all, to recognize that each of them reveals something about who I am as writer.

In "A Case for Writing While Black," Sherrie Fernandez-Williams says, "My personal commitment as a writer is to never utter the words, *I am a writer who happens to be a black woman.* Instead, I will emphatically declare without hesitation that *I am a black woman writer*, and I will place my story squarely within the black cultural and historical context where it belongs" (qtd. in Lee 31). Each writer must determine the identity they will claim and the community in which they wish to place themselves.

Readings: These readings offer inspiration for considering how you are perceived as a writer, the factors that influence your work, the way you define yourself as a writer, and how you think of your writing community.

> "Cadence" in *Geographies of Light* by Lisa Suhair Majaj
> "And Are You a Latina Writer?" in *Woman in Front of the Sun* by Judith Ortiz Cofer

"Cadence" by Lisa Suhair Majaj reveals the struggle of being pulled between two cultures and their expectations. Part of the audience views her through the lens of the "exotic" while the other views her as "compatriot" (65). The pressure to choose one side, to be viewed as one thing is what the poet must resist if she is to find her voice and speak from a position that encompasses her whole identity and allows her to move between her cultures, a space that Majaj describes as being "Two cultures can be lighter than one/if the space between them is fluid" (66). Speaking her own voice becomes an act of resistance against both sets of expectations and a way to articulate the truth of her place in both cultures.

In "And Are You a Latina Writer?," Judith Ortiz Cofer addresses some of the same issues as Majaj's poem regarding external expectations and where the writer chooses to place herself. Claiming English as her literary language, Ortiz Cofer rejects the notion that she should be writing in Spanish. For many of us, being educated in the U.S. means that English is the language we have learned to use in our writing, and we must claim it as our own. Having grown up for much of her life outside of a Puerto Rican community, Ortiz Cofer recognizes that geographical distance is not the same as cultural distance. Her culture exists within her, and while community is of importance, it is not a requirement for writing out of one's cultural identity. Like Majaj, she lays claim to both cultures and rejects the notion of being only one thing: "My mission as an emerging writer became to use my art as a bridge. ... I would be crossing the bridge of my design and construction, at will, not abandoning either side, but traveling back and forth without fear and confusion as to where I belonged—I belong to both" (109). Claiming both cultural identities becomes a place of empowerment for Ortiz Cofer as a writer.

As multicultural writers, our work and our identities are intricately intertwined. David Mura says, "When a person comes from a family or a group that has been marginalized, when she is one of the 'subalterns,' the silence such a person confronts about herself and her experiences within the greater culture is a political condition. In such cases, the very act of writing about herself and her experiences becomes a political act" (Mura 13). When we put our words on paper, we participate in an act of resistance by claiming ourselves and our place in the world.

If Education Is Not Multicultural, It Isn't Education

Chrystos

In this piece, I'll speak as an individual colonized person, not as the "voice of Indigenous people," even though this is often foisted upon me. The idea that one person could represent an entire series of groups is a colonizer proposition in which I have no interest. I am speaking into the roar of misogyny & white supremacy, two of the founding principles of the usa. I don't know to whom I am speaking & so I'm also speaking into a void. I use my life experience to guide me through. I have found that almost all non-Indigenous people (not only Caucasians) are ignorant of & usually indifferent to Indian Country. Only in the last ten years have we been added to the list of "minorities" here. We were even famously omitted by President Obama in a major speech. I find the word "minorities" very offensive, a reduction, as though not ALL of us are equals before the law—as indeed, we are not. Much of this land is legally ours (through violated treaties) and all of it, morally so. I myself have never met a "minor" person. This is simply left-over bad language. Lest you complain that these introductory words are "too political," I'll assert that every word is always political, often by omission, as in "mankind" (which I call "mancruel," which is more accurate). All writing is political, even by omission, even murder mysteries, which propose that people will kill each other for profit. These are

Chrystos
Tacoma, WA, USA

considered "light reading," but they establish that greed is the dominant trait of humans, which is a profound philosophical statement. I read & enjoy murder mysteries, particularly because they prove my "political point" vis-à-vis greed. Everything which I find abhorrent—rape, torture, sexual abuse, theft, war, murder—is motivated by the sin of greed. While I remain uncertain if it is indeed "the dominant human trait," it is certainly the main thrust of colonization. This is not a post-colonial world, as scholars like to opine. None of our colonizers have left or conceded power. India & parts of Africa are post-colonial, but not the usa or canada.

Indigenous culture was transmitted orally & carefully, not necessarily with an individual point of view. Translating across this different way of seeing & living is a complex task. An excellent illustration of this is the novel, *Noopiming: The Cure for White Ladies.*

This essay is a colonizer act & each word I write could affect future generations. I write with them in mind. While many Indigenous people now speak English as our primary language, we are not speaking the "Queen's English." We don't agree that "Queen" is a good idea. Nor "King." The principles on which the usa was founded are based on the Iroquois Confederacy. Our idea is that kings are useless. There is a silly motto that betrays the actual intent of the usa—"Every man's home is his castle." So, most people have come here (with the exception of enslaved Africans) in order to "be kings," rather than to participate in a democracy. It is always useful to point out that in the original greek democracy women were not allowed to vote or speak in public & they held slaves. I would posit that the usa has never been a democracy, even now, as we have sex slavery traffic running through our ports (& some homes). Thus, we find ourselves in the current mess of "sovereign citizens," one of many useless phrases.

The world is changing around us, as she always has & I believe the future will discard autocracy in all its many forms. Learning does not happen from 9 to 3 in carefully planned slots. This is always happening every moment. How we treat others, that is, with or without respect, informs whether they will learn from us. Our actions are more powerful than lectures. To be a good teacher means that one actually sees those one is teaching, their actual selves, not one's preconceived ideas of them. & of course, a crucial aspect of teaching is learning to learn from your students. Nothing I can say about teaching is as important as the relationship you can choose to have with your students. Not as "pals," because one cannot be friends across lines of power, but as fellow humans. Because colonization teaches us to look down our noses at others, to prevent human bonding, which is dangerous to those with "power over," the act of treating another human *as* human is a lifelong struggle.

The world we now face, of climate uncertainty & pandemic, constrains our ability to trust one another, even more so than previously. Your students will learn nothing useful from you if they don't trust you.

Each of us can write well by using the usual tools. Reading widely from many countries & cultures. Focusing in on a subject with research. Learning the basics: using the seven senses—usual plus humor & Spirit; alliteration; rhymes; repetition; rhythm; homophones; etc.

The development of a distinct voice requires being in communion with one's soul & history & place, which is a different journey for everyone. While all of us should develop the skills to write clearly (which requires being able to think clearly), not everyone will be a great writer. This is actually not "teachable." Or rather, those of us who write, teach ourselves. The best gift one can give a young writer is space & encouragement. Many young people of color have never been allowed to have time to think about what they want to say and so that time is crucial to give. Writing tools don't need to be mysterious. Writing is, after all, only speaking on paper. If you can talk, you can write.

My own writing life is mostly a matter of listening to my mind & recording. A line pops into my head (often very inconveniently) & when I stop to write down those few words, the rest follows. One has to work to be able to hear one's mind in the riot of noise which is our present circumstances. Being alone & quiet is a great boon. When I hear that "ping," I know "here we go." Some days pass with me only whining in my journal (which I recommend, as whining often leads to something useful), then 3 poems in a day. I've learned to trust myself & don't bother to worry about "writer's block" which recreates itself, much like insomnia.

The obstacles to my writing all rest in the publishing world, with which I have had a contentious relationship. Frequently there have been attempts to censor me (successful in the beginning), or Indigenous writers are often ignored altogether (less so now). I should mention that all the attempts to censor me were from feminist publishers & always having to do with "sex roles," the sex war, etc. There are feminist rules & talking points & taboos as in all groups. Perhaps my biggest problem is my own tongue which can be quite sharp when thwarted. I once wrote a 14page letter in defense of a last line which they printed perhaps solely because they were intimidated (concerned prostitution—an ongoing point of contention).

My greatest asset is that I was invisible as I grew up & had the opportunity to form my own mind. I've always written for myself, to understand my own circumstances. Approval is not my goal. I do want to approve of myself, but everyone else is just noises off. I've written against a tide of disapproval from my family, which is a great boost of freedom. It is often difficult to hear oneself in the cacophony of parents. I have thousands of unpublished poems laying around all over because, while writing (in longhand) is crucial—publishing is a pain in the ass. I hate to type.

I often write on whatever is handy—napkins, used envelopes, backs of books I'm reading, and once, memorably on a placemat in an IHOP. I'm trying to organize my papers so as not to saddle this onus on my long-suffering spouse, but I end up writing about what I find, which makes ever more paper. About the only thing more interesting to me than my own mind is leaves, stones, branches. Sometimes I despair that I'll never shut up. Sunny jokes she expects to hear from me about whether I like the inside of my coffin. Still, all & all, I've had a very good time playing around with English. The only useful editor I've ever had was Gloria Anzaldúa.

I experiment always when writing—I think of english as a toy, a somewhat malicious toy, but I like exploding clichés, popular culture, notions of what is proper; seeing how many times I can repeat a letter, using homophones, shapes of the poem on paper, twisting the meaning of words until they break & so on.

Some books I'll highly recommend are *The Way to Rainy Mountain* (Momaday), *She Had Some Horses* (Harjo), *Earthquake Weather* (Gould), *I'll Sing to the Day I Die* (Brant), *Sula* (Morrison), anything by Gloria Anzaldúa, Audre Lorde, James Baldwin, & so on. Drew Hayden Taylor has a great sense of humor which would appeal to teenagers. Actually, I suggest that you Google Indigenous Authors & spend a summer with us to make your own choices. In order to teach multiculturally, you yourself have to be widely read in all the literatures available. We're in a Renaissance! Enjoy yourself.

Chrystos I started out as an angry young dyke fighting for justice. Now, I'm an old dyke doing the same.

The Curriculum: How I Learned to Be a Writer

Susan Muaddi Darraj

In elementary school, I read Lucy Maude Montgomery's novels and fell in love with Anne, the curious girl with red hair who loved rich language as much as she loved Gilbert Blythe. I adored her spunk and her intellect, and all I wished for was carrot-red hair and fields and valleys and rivers to discover (living in a crammed row house in South Philadelphia, with a backyard the size of a postage stamp, I could only imagine spending summers roaming around a farm).

In middle school, my tastes ran darker, to cyanide and stabbings and conspiratorial murders on locomotives. Every time I entered our town's small library building, the librarian smiled at me. She knew I was on a mission to read every book ever written by Agatha Christie; I was so successful that I read most of them twice. Reading Christie made me feel like a sophisticated adult, especially when it meant I could watch the PBS versions of Hercule Poirot and Miss Marple. (Anything delivered in a British accent felt sophisticated when you were thirteen, especially in a home where "village Arabic" mingled with "urban English.")

In high school, I discovered Virginia Woolf before the curriculum introduced her to me. I'd expressed an interest in "feminist writers," and so a teacher recommended Woolf. After reading some of Woolf's work, I remember looking for the "angel in the house"—I was intent on defying her and her oppression (whoever she was). I imagined that I, too, was living in a society that wanted to stop me

S. M. Darraj (✉)
Johns Hopkins University, Baltimore, MD, USA
e-mail: Smuaddi1@jhu.edu

P. Kaldas, *Writing the Multicultural Experience*,
https://doi.org/10.1007/978-3-031-06124-0_14

from writing, even though my working-class parents, upon hearing I wanted to be a writer, had purchased a typewriter for me as a gift.

The bottom line was this: I'd known since fourth grade that I wanted to be a writer, so when I read Montgomery, Christie, Woolf, and others, I read them strategically. Not only was I looking for an enjoyable story, I was searching for what people now refer to as "mentor texts." In my reading, I focused on plot, character, setting, and *themes*. In that sense, I followed the learning pattern of my immigrant parents as they assimilated to life in the U.S.: Watch other people who seem to know what they're doing, emulate them, assess your smallest efforts, and stick to it.

As a result, my early stories were silly and naive, but they had structure, they had dialogue, and they hit all the elements of plot. What else was there?

Of course, emerging writers don't know what they don't know. And I didn't know that I was missing something crucial. I began to understand that gap when I entered college, as a first-generation student, and signed up as an English major. Who imagined that you could get an A for simply reading books that you enjoyed, discussing how and why they worked, and then attempting to write something similar yourself? This college thing was new and uncertain, but I was winning.

There, I discovered Toni Morrison and Sandra Cisneros. And I was stunned. Later, in graduate school, the work of Esmeralda Santiago and Alice Walker entered into and changed my life.

> By the time I read June Jordan, I was a new person altogether.
> Because now I knew that writing was more than plot, character, and setting.
> Now, I was focused on something riveting. Compelling. I'd glimpsed the thing that grabbed the reader's hand and sat them down beside the narrator to listen attentively.
> I was focused on voice.
> Specifically, my voice.

I still have quotes from all of these writers tacked up around my writing desk. There is one by June Jordan, in "Poem About My Rights," which taught me about strength and claiming my identity:

> I am not wrong: Wrong is not my name
> My name is my own my own my own
> and I can't tell you who the hell set things up like this
> but I can tell you that from now on my resistance
> my simple and daily and nightly self-determination
> may very well cost you your life.

The power that erupted from these words. The confidence that ricocheted in my heart when I read them, like a mantra. These women, people said, wrote from what is commonly referred to as "the margins," although it felt like they'd formed a firing squad on those margins and aimed their words at the center of my confused heart.

They showed me a way to express myself.
And who was I, anyway?

Let me first state who I *had been*: an Arab American daughter of immigrants who thought "literature" was a space occupied by white characters, created by white writers. Silly, but true. My early stories were filled with Heathers and Jennifers. In *Bad Feminist*, Roxane Gay writes about her love of the Sweet Valley High book series: "Some experiences are universal. A girl is a girl, whether she lives in West Omaha or Sweet Valley." I agree with Gay in one sense; I, too, stretched my imagination to make myself fit white worlds. I could be Anne, running around Prince Edward Island, or Nancy Drew, chasing thieves while wearing a skirt and a neckerchief. But it went farther with me—I thought these were the only lives that warranted being in books.

When I became aware that brown and Black women were also writing literature—what a silly thought, it seems like now—I bought all their books and made them my mentors.

Because I had become someone new. I had become a writer. (Of literature, thank you very much.)

In fact, June Jordan's poem, "Moving Towards Home," was the first time I'd ever seen the Palestinian experience expressed in an American poem: "I was born a Black woman/and now/I am become a Palestinian. … It is time to make our way home." I understood that the best writing was a generous act, a reaching out, an expression of love and solidarity. The best writing took your hand and said, "I am with you." In her article, "June Jordan's Songs of Palestine," Therese Saliba writes, "For Arab feminists of my generation, June Jordan brought us out of our invisibility. She embodied transnational feminist solidarity long before it was in vogue."

In the curriculum I cobbled together over several years, by reading women of color, I understood so much about writing, including *how* to actually do it. In her essay, "Furor Scribendi," Octavia Butler wrote,

First forget inspiration. Habit is more dependable. Habit will sustain you whether you're inspired or not. Habit will help you finish and polish your stories. Inspiration won't. Habit is persistence in practice. You don't start out writing good stuff. You start out writing crap and thinking it's good stuff, and then gradually you get better at it. That's why I say one of the most valuable traits is persistence.

This advice synched with my immigrant upbringing, where persistence was key to anything: finding work, learning English, building savings. In other words, the path to becoming a writer was something already ingrained in me.

When my children were very young, I realized that writing was a luxury. I didn't have a room of my own, as Woolf had admonished me to do so many years ago. The room I wrote in had two cribs in it and a playpen, and a recliner chair for nursing. I was lucky if I could read while feeding a baby. The physical stress of working full-time and raising children threatened to overwhelm me at times, as I had no spare money to hire nannies, sitters, cleaners, or other services to make the load easier. I ended every day with the same thought: *I did it. But how the hell am I going to do it again tomorrow?*

Habit, Butler replied. Get into a habit. And stick to it.

The only "regular" times I had were in the morning, from 5:00 am to 6:30 am. That's when the babies would start to wake up. That was when I had to get them up, diapered, changed, fed, and loaded into the car seats for the drive to the daycare attached to my work building. Six thirty in the morning, when the first gurgle of an awakening baby was heard, signaled the start to a roller coaster day, a day that would not stop until 10:00 pm or later.

So, it had to be 5:00 am. I set my alarm, got up, made coffee, and stared at my notebook for ninety minutes.

> I did that every day until I finally started to write something
> It worked.

I have awakened almost every day, including weekends and holidays, and even while on vacation, to honor my writing hours. I may not write seven days a week, but during my writing hours (currently 5:00 am to 7:00 am), I do something that is related to my writing career: edit some pages, write new ones, compose an email to my agent, read current books in my genre, and more. In this manner, I have published over a dozen books, including two short story collections and four children's novels.

A co-worker said to me, not long ago, "I used to be jealous of you and how productive you are, until I learned that you got up so early to write. I guess that makes sense now, because I would never do that. I'd rather sleep."

I respect that feeling. We all need sleep. I sleep too, but a little earlier in the evening and for about 60 fewer minutes than others. It may not be the best way, but it's the way I've chosen and it works.

There is the famous quote from Toni Morrison, the one everyone recites. The one that was repeated on my Facebook and social media feeds for days and weeks after her death in August of 2019: "If there's a book that you want to read, but it hasn't been written yet, then you must write it."

It is the quote that, later, would inspire me to write an entire book series.

Several years ago, when I'd already published a couple of short story collections, my daughter unexpectedly dropped a new task onto my plate. She was reading Anne of Green Gables, and we were watching the new miniseries on Netflix together. We both talked about Anne's bravery and her spunk and her curiosity. A girl who would ask a question of anybody. A girl whose curiosity led her to adventures every single day. But what my daughter said to me was: how come there weren't books about girls like Anne, but who were also Arab, like us?

The pain that bubbled up from that question was not revealed to me until a couple of days later. Instead, it lingered with me and bothered me like a newly forming poison ivy rash. I could feel it spreading, growing more and more irritating. What was going on in my heart? What had that question triggered within me?

The answer revealed itself a few days later when I was looking for books with Arab girls for my daughter. I found the novel *Habibi* by Naomi Shihab Nye, the first children's novel I'd read with an Arab character; I remembered it had not been published until I was in college myself.

My daughter's question bothered me because it was the same question I had harbored in my heart for years when I'd been her age. Except, back then, I didn't have the visual horizon to even understand that books with Arab characters could even exist, much less that I could write them.

Where are the Arab girls? Why has the publishing industry disappeared us?

Toni Morrison gave me an answer, though. There was something I could do about it.

Writing the book was actually easier than I thought. You may never find a writer to admit that to you. It wasn't just easy. It was pure joy.

I thought about my character. I decided she would be filled with joy and so I called her Farah.

I wondered what kinds of conflict she would face. What kind of dramatic action could I give her? This would be the first book series with a Palestinian character in it after all. Maybe I could have my character face some kind of discrimination. Maybe she could be bullied at school for being Arab, the way I had been.

Then I read Denene Millner's pivotal op-ed in *The New York Times*, "Black Kids Don't Want to Read About Harriet Tubman All the Time." Millner says:

The "diverse" books making it to the shelves aren't very diverse at all. With few exceptions, the same stories are being told again and again, fed to children like some bowl of dry, lumpy oatmeal with just a sprinkle of brown sugar to make it go down a little easier.

The typical children's picture books featuring black characters focus on the degradation and endurance of our people. You can fill nearly half the bookshelves in the Schomburg with children's books about the civil rights movement, slavery, basketball players and musicians, and various "firsts." These stories consistently paint African-Americans as the aggrieved and the conquerors, the agitators and the superheroes who fought for their right to be recognized as full human beings.

Millner agrees that these books are important, but that Black children also need books that portray the magic of their experiences. She writes that young Black readers "want to read books that engage with their everyday experiences, featuring characters who look like them. Just like any other child."

In the kidlit world, we have a term for books that always focus on the marginalization and oppression of marginalized and oppressed communities: "crisis literature." It's almost like these communities need to be reminded that they have not had a fair deal in this world.

As an author new to kidlit, I examined my initial instinct to make my character face some kind of traumatic action. Wasn't I doing to Arab girls exactly what the publishing and the media industries had always been doing? Depicting us in dramatic situations? Putting us in crisis? Defining us by our struggles?

No, I thought, this was going to be a book that was joyous. There would be conflict. There would be a bully. But none of the issues in the book would center on Farah's ethnic identity. In fact, I thought going even further: Farah, my girl, would live in a sort of diverse utopia in which many of her friends came from immigrant families. She would speak Arabic at home, English at school, and move seamlessly between two worlds. This would not cause her any kind of problem or conflict whatsoever.

My daughter has read Anne of Green Gables. She likes the *Babysitter's Club* and Nancy Drew, and we have watched some of the new Hercule Poirot films together. In addition, she has read all four books of *Farah Rocks*, a book series written by her mother, who finally found her voice.

Susan Muaddi Darraj won an American Book Award in 2016 for her novel-in-stories, *A Curious Land*. She has also been awarded a Ford Fellowship, a Maryland State Arts Council Award, and two Arab American Book Awards. Her book series, FARAH ROCKS, is the first series to feature a Palestinian American protagonist, the funny and brave Farah Hajjar. Susan lives in Baltimore, Maryland, and teaches in the MA in Writing program at the Johns Hopkins University. Follow her on Twitter/Instagram @SusanDarraj.

Imaginary Homelands and Moveable Feasts: An Indian Diaspora Woman Writer's Perspective

Balli Kaur Jaswal

"How are we to live in the world?" asks Salman Rushdie in his essay "Imaginary Homelands" (Rushdie 18). It is a question posed to and about South Asian diaspora writers, speaking to the complexity of our "plural and partial" identities and how we bring history, exile, and a legacy of migrant aspirations onto the page (Rushdie 15). Rushdie suggests that physical alienation from India inspires fantasies of India within the minds of migrants, to help them cope with this sense of loss (Rushdie 10). However, like many feminist South Asian writers, I find Rushdie's concept of imaginary homelands incomplete because it does not take into account the experiences of women in the diaspora. In "Women, Homelands and the Indian Diaspora," Nandi Bhatia argues that "Imaginary Homelands" contains little consideration for how India's cultural values continue to define and control gender roles. In constructing the imaginary homeland as a way of coping with the trauma of exile, the (male) migrant's search for identity is rooted in patriarchal cultural systems, says Bhatia, who describes these idealized narratives about the homeland as "regressive mechanisms that seek to structure women's lives" (Bhatia 512).

Indeed, in the 1960s and 1970s, South Asian migration to Western countries was considered a "male phenomenon" (Jayaram 23); after the 1990s,

B. K. Jaswal (✉)
Yale-NUS College, Singapore, Singapore
e-mail: ballijaswal@yale-nus.edu.sg

more women with professional skills and higher degrees migrated independently (Sheth 128). The emergence of women's voices in South Asian diaspora
fiction revealed a gendered experience of the migrant narrative. If men create
imaginary homelands that romanticize the patriarchal system that they left
behind, then female writers also create an idealized world through fiction
where they seek to control their narratives and develop autonomous identities. Further distinguishing the difference between female and male narratives
in South Asian diaspora fiction, Somdatta Mandal observes that the women
are "in a state of permanent migrancy and they transform the pain of disloca-
tion into a celebration where exile helps them to discover new territories of
experience" (Mandal 88). Women's writing is celebratory not necessarily
because women always triumph in these narratives, but because the migrant
journey is redefined through a female lens.

I write fiction about South Asian diaspora women to create narratives that
show women succeeding at challenging multiple hierarchies. In an analysis of
South Asian image and identity, critic Lisa Lau describes the writing process
for South Asian women writers as "a negotiation of a space ... to write, rewrite,
re-define, re-name, and re-invent, in a traditionally and proudly patriarchal
society and culture" (Lau 38). Novels by Anita Desai, Bharati Mukherjee,
Amulya Malladi, Kiran Desai, and Sunetra Gupta are prime examples of such
narratives. Jhumpa Lahiri's collection *Interpreter of Maladies* explores the
immigrant experience and all of its ensuing challenges—alienation, intergen-
erational conflicts, racism—and situates them in the varied experiences of
women who strive for independence and equality. Works of South Asian
immigrant fiction set in the U.K.—namely *Gifted* by Nikita Lalwani, *Life Isn't
All Ha Ha Hee Hee* by Meera Syal, and *Brick Lane* by Monica Ali—also explore
women's familial and societal roles. The struggle against double colonization
is a significant theme in these narratives (Hedge 89). They highlight the plight
of fighting two layers of oppression: misogyny of South Asian cultural norms
that value men over women, and racism of post-colonial societies where
Western values are perceivably threatened by an influx of immigrants.

My 2019 novel *The Unlikely Adventures of the Shergill Sisters* was an attempt
to join my fellow South Asian female authors in claiming a space for women's
narratives in a culture that dismisses our voices. Following three British-Indian
sisters on a pilgrimage to India to fulfill their mother's last wishes, the novel
portrays the contemporary Indian woman's existence in the world, and inves-
tigates how the lingering effects of post-colonialism and Indian nationalism
factor into her ethnic and gender identity. Although the sisters are on the
journey together, each must endure a rite of passage in the tradition of South

Asian women novelists like Anita Desai and Nayantara Sehgal, who use their female protagonists' conflicts with oppressive cultural values to mark their "transformation from weakness to strength and from restriction to freedom" (Hussain 56). The sisters' journey also highlights the impact of migration on women and the power of the homeland to both attract and repel first-generation immigrants.

When *The Unlikely Adventures of the Shergill Sisters* was published in the U.S. and the U.K., I experienced the common sense of disassociation that many authors feel as their narratives are packaged as consumer products. As a South Asian woman writer, I had particular concerns about authenticity and representation: now that the story was out of my hands, would the publishers accurately reflect the experiences of Indian women in their marketing materials? These anxieties had plagued me while writing the early drafts of the novel as well. While some authors seek to create nuanced narratives about minority experiences, Western audiences are more interested in portrayals of differences that distinctly set minority stories apart from so-called mainstream narratives. Although minority representations have diversified since South Asian diaspora literature first started emerging in the market in the late twentieth century, continuing the narrative of "otherness" is still an expectation of minority writing.

The "commodification of ethnic difference," says critic Tamara Bhalla, is particularly problematic for women writing about this subject matter (Bhalla 81). Tropes that emphasize South Asians' cultural differences, such as arranged marriages or the taboos around interracial dating, are gendered because of how those stories are classified in the literary market. Book covers are a clear indicator. "In this arena, male authors' work tends to be coded as serious, literary, intellectual and historical, while that of female authors is sexualised, exoticised and stereotyped" (Bhalla 81). The devaluing of South Asian women's narratives can be attributed to the legacies of two crucial historical movements: British colonialism and Indian nationalism. Justifying their mission in the name of civilization, British colonists highlighted the oppression of women under Indian tradition. The self-preserving reaction from Indian nationalists was to emphasize and maintain the spiritual qualities of Indian women that could not be conquered by the West (Chatterjee 119–121). Dually oppressed under white imperialism and Indian patriarchy, the South Asian woman writing for a Western audience is burdened with the responsibility of maintaining authenticity, but her narrative is often only accepted if "oppression and victimisation of the Diaspora" are dominant themes (Parameswaran 33).

The sheer diversity of the South Asian diaspora, with its multitudes of cultures, traditions, and languages, defies such stereotyping in literature. Yet simplified narratives about Indian immigrants are often sought as a form of touristic escapism through which readers can experience a reality that is distinctly removed from their own. In the interests of packaging narratives as sellable products, publishers peddle the convenient idea of a monolithic Indian identity, one that writer Namrata Poddar describes as "moot" because it doesn't exist, just as one American reality doesn't exist (Poddar 94). In "The Language of Power and the Power of Language," Lisa Lau holds writers somewhat responsible by suggesting that Indian writers writing in English are limited by the Western audience's perception of this monolithic identity. They avoid creating nuances that represent regional identities, instead choosing to highlight themes that are associated with a broader notion of "Indianness" (Lau 32–33).

Whatever the reasons for the formation of this monolithic Indian identity presented in fiction, the results are especially problematic for South Asian women writers, who must carve out space in a context where they are marginalized by both race and gender. Feminist scholar Uma Narayan describes these women's roles as "emissaries," "mirrors," or "the authentic insiders" (Narayan 127)—all roles that inevitably result in tokenism because these writers are given the impossible challenge of compressing the Indian identity into a single narrative. Writers are pigeonholed and less willing to take artistic risks out of fear of being "condemned as being inaccurate authors" (Lau 39).

There is also a further danger of confusing exoticness with multiculturalism. In his essay, "The Postcolonial Exotic," literary critic Graham Huggan observes that the continued peddling of exotic tropes in publishing is a bottom line decision—exoticism sells. The sense of wonder and opportunity for escapism invoked by such narratives comes with another dangerous assumption, that reading such narratives is an act of appreciation of cultural diversity. "Exoticism relieves its practitioners, however, from the burdensome task of actually learning about 'other' cultures" (Huggan 26).

How do I avoid a monolithic depiction of Indian women? How do I maintain authenticity in my writing? I start a work by examining my characters' core values. These values may be shaped somewhat by their cultural contexts, but it is not their job to teach or promote anything. They just need to exist in all their messy, complicated dimensions. Characters are less likely to become stand-ins for particular arguments or viewpoints once they become complex individuals who could walk right off the page. Considering the form and purpose of fiction is important—the main objective of telling a story is immersing a reader in another person's life and experiencing the world as them. I never start a story with the aim of making an argument. That is what speeches and op-eds are for; there is nothing more grating on a reader than polemic poorly disguised as storytelling. The same rules apply to other components of the narrative: dialogue must advance the plot and the character development; it is not there to educate the reader about the migrant experience. Descriptions of setting should immerse the reader in the place—they do not need to resemble a Lonely Planet guide. This isn't to say that the cultural teachings that occur from reading fiction are accidental or unwanted, but they should not be the deliberate focus of the work.

When I began writing *The Unlikely Adventures of the Shergill Sisters*, I wanted to explore how the tension between tradition and modernity influences the identities of South Asian diaspora women. My initial character sketches and notes were an early attempt to create characters that each represented a respective archetype of the traditional, modern, and moderate woman. However, as the storyline developed, the characters revealed multiplicities and contradictions that became the more pertinent and intriguing source of tension for the narrative. I took inspiration from the nuances in Meera Syal's characterization of the three protagonists in *Life Isn't All Ha Ha Hee Hee*: rather than presenting the British-Indian identity as a problem that the characters would resolve by the end of the novel, Syal used their experiences to unearth more complex (and sometimes unanswerable) questions about identity. The fluidity of the women's identities shows them in a permanent state of existing between worlds. As Syal's character Tania explains: "We meet the world head up, head on, we meet our men and we bow down gratefully, cling to compromise like a lover who promises all will be well if we don't make trouble. We hear our mothers' voices and we heed them, to make up for all the other imagined transgressions in our lives. Everything else I can pick up or discard when I choose; my culture is a moveable feast" (Syal 147–148).

As descriptors of cultural values in narratives about Indian women, "traditional" and "modern" tend to be simplified and pitted against each other as diametric opposites. Lau warns against ascribing judgment to these values: "In a search for cultural purity, too many fall into the unrealistic assumption that tradition is at polar opposites from modernity, seeking to designate one as desirable and the other as undesirable" (253). In order to create characters who would withstand the challenges of the pilgrimage and contribute to a satisfying and authentic narrative arc, I needed to explore "the selectivity of the culture which diasporic South Asians live and practice" because it reminds readers of the inherent complexities and contradictions within this identity in a "reinvented culture" (Lau 255). The tension between tradition and modernity had to exist *within* each woman rather than as an external metric of cultural identity.

When considering the challenges of depicting the minority experience authentically in my own writing, I turn to the works of Nigerian author Chimamanda Ngozi Adichie. In her TED Talk, "The Danger of the Single Story," Adichie explains that certain power structures in the media that disseminate information from West to East enable the West to have multiple narratives, while the East is perceived in very one-dimensional ways. She uses an anecdote to make this comparison clear: "I recently spoke at a university where a student told me it was such a shame that Nigerian men were physical abusers like the father character in my novel. I told him that I had recently read a novel called *American Psycho*, and that it was a shame that young Americans were serial murderers" (Adichie).

In her short story, "Jumping Monkey Hill," Adichie explores the conflicts that arise when writing about middle class Africa in a Western context. Set in South Africa, the story follows a Nigerian writer named Ujunwa who notices and becomes uncomfortable with the deliberate emphasis on exoticism of an African writers' retreat run by a British man. From the start of the story, Ujunwa observes how the resort has been curated to fit an inauthentic and touristic ideal of Africa: "The resort had the complacence of the well fed about it ... she imagined affluent foreign tourists would dart around taking pictures of lizards and then return home still unaware that there were more black people than red-capped lizards in South Africa" (Adichie 95). The owner's wife comments on Ujunwa's "exquisite bone structure" and asks if she came from royal stock in Nigeria, tempting Ujunwa to ask (although she doesn't) if she "ever needed royal blood to explain the good looks of friends back in London" (Adichie 99). In this exchange, Adichie demonstrates a power imbalance in assumptions of beauty between Western and African women. Instead of allowing Ujunwa to fully accept the assumption, she shows her working toward an equalizing parallel.

However, the imbalance persists between Ujunwa and the Western patrons of the writing retreat. When she is writing her short story, she considers a "common" name for her character versus an "exotic" one (Adichie 100). At dinner, Edward, the British leader of the retreat, tells her that ostrich is a staple of African cuisine even though it is not representative of the cuisine that Ujunwa is familiar with. The writing workshops run by Edward highlight the Western policing of African narratives. In response to a Senegalese woman's story about a lesbian daughter coming out to her parents, "Edward chewed at his pipe thoughtfully before he said that homosexual stories of this sort weren't reflective of Africa, really" (Adichie 107–108). Ujunwa blurts out, "Which

Africa (Adichie 108)?" Later, Edward praises another participant's story, which contains familiar tropes of the expected African narrative—militiamen and violence in the Congo (Adichie 109). Ujunwa's observation is that the story reads like something from *The Economist*, with stock characters (Adichie 109). Adichie subverts power structures by creating a character who questions and challenges the traditional narratives. Ujunwa's resistance against a certain kind of African story perpetuated by Western readers mirrors Adichie's own journey to diversify narratives from that continent.

The writing workshop scene in Adichie's story reflects my early experiences as an Indian writer in predominantly white American spaces in my undergraduate years. My classmates showed disproportionate interest in the exotic locales of my stories, with some commenting about the "magic realism" of a scene in a crowded marketplace in Singapore that was in fact completely realistic. The suspicion about the inauthenticity of my stories when I mentioned familiar American brands like "Pepsi" and "Formica," was superseded only by gratification and delight at terms like "sugarcane juice" and "karang guni." I learned that difference and novelty were rewarded, while familiarity was unsettling—my culture and locale needed to remain inscrutable in order to be considered worthy.

My earliest experiences with diaspora fiction were from an era when American and British publishers were tentatively making space for Indian writing. In the late 1990s and early 2000s, these novels depicted Indian women as suffering, naïve, and one-dimensional characters. Critic Ashish Gupta made this observation in a critique of a 2007 *New Yorker* issue, which highlighted writing from the Indian subcontinent. "The fact that *The New Yorker* was billed as a 'fiction issue' seemed no excuse for parading the standard line-up of beggars, charlatans, greedy medical graduates, defecators on the riverbank, etc. ... What gets published remains a function of neo-colonial instincts ... and who gets published is a verdict, not on artistic integrity, but on how well one's sensibilities have been sharpened by colonial benchmarks of education and perception" (Ashish Gupta 44–45).

India was also often represented as an antithesis of the West. In "Indian Traditions and the Western Imagination," Amartya Sen views these portrayals as colonial remnants where "distancing" Indian culture from the so-called mainstream of Western traditions maintain a classification system that presents India as exotic, otherworldly, and wondrous (Sen 2). These narratives traded heavily on Edward Said's concept of Orientalism—the relationship "power, of domination, of varying degrees of a complex hegemony" between East and West (Said 1994). Although Said's Orientalist is not necessarily a Westerner, he makes it clear that the Orientalist trades in inauthentic representation because he is disengaged with its complexities and realities, only seeking to portray the Orient as a subsidiary culture to the Occident. "He is never concerned with the Orient except as the first cause of what he says. What he says and writes, by virtue of the fact that it is said or written is meant to indicate that the Orientalist is outside the Orient, both as an existential and moral fact" (Said 2006). Said's broad definition of the Orientalist as an outsider suggests that Eastern writers are also culpable of promoting Orientalist narratives if their work continues the Orientalist tradition of portraying a superficial image of the East for the benefit of Western readers. Lau holds Orientalism responsible for exoticizing narratives, but she also points to natural human perception of difference: "[What] is commonplace in India, for example, may be to a reader ignorant of Indian ways, a piece of writing which is particularly perceptive or extraordinarily insightful. It may be that novelty and difference is the charm of the literature to a western readership" (Lau 40).

Diasporas by their very nature are spaces of diverse identities, complex hierarchies, and shifting loyalties, and these narratives remind readers of the individual experiences that challenge the monolithic perception of South Asian immigrants. *The Unlikely Adventures of the Shergill Sisters* came from my desire to add to this collective history and to continue creating nuance in our stories of return, belonging, and acceptance. Fiction might be the most suitable realm for exploring the real life issues that South Asian diaspora women face. Characters and their behaviors are framed in contexts of colonialism, migration, and gender imbalances, giving readers a complex understanding of the conditions that create the dual oppression of South Asian diaspora women, and their effects on those women's identities. The characters come of age in the context of frameworks designed to keep them subjugated, but as they fight for autonomy over their narratives, they become reborn as women who are wholly themselves despite the archetypes imposed upon them. Critic Savita Goel says, "The endeavour to write a novel about one's native country on the basis of memory has been an irresistible challenge and a compelling necessity for a number of exiled or immigrant writers who have been cut off from their ethnic roots" (Goel 189). My endeavor was to heal this sense of being removed from the homeland, and to create a link between the past and present through an exploration of the lives of fictional women whose values and experiences were familiar to mine. The "compelling necessity" led the book from its early roots as a response to male-dominated narratives of India, to a process of discovery about the multifarious identities of women of the South Asian diaspora.

Works Cited

Adichie, Chimamanda Ngozi. "The danger of a single story." Filmed July 2009a at TEDGlobal 2009, Oxford University, UK. Video, 10:43.

Adichie, Chimamanda Ngozi. "Jumping Monkey Hill." In *The Thing Around Your Neck*, by Chimamanda Ngozi Adichie, 95–115. London: Fourth Estate, 2009b.

Bhatia, Nandi. "Women, Homelands, and the Indian Diaspora." *The Centennial Review* 42, no. 3 (Fall 1998): 511–526.

Chatterjee, Partha. *The Nation and Its Fragments: Colonial and Postcolonial Histories.* Princeton, NJ: Princeton University Press, 1993.

Goel, Savitha. "A Literary Voyage to India: Rohinton Mistry's *A Fine Balance.*" In *Writers of the Indian Diaspora: Theory and Practice*, edited by Jasbir Jain, 189–198. Jaipur: Rawat Publications, 1998.

Gupta, Ashish. "The Extraordinary Composition of the Expatriate Writer." In *Writers of the Indian Diaspora: Essays on Culture and Identity*, edited by Jasbir Jain, 44–45. Jaipur: Rawat Publications, 1998.

Huggan, Graham. "The Postcolonial Exotic." *Transition*, no. 64 (1994): 22–29.

Jayaram, Nayarama. *The Indian Diaspora: Dynamics of Migration*. New Delhi: Sage Publications, 2004.

Lau, Lisa. "The Language of Power and the Power of Language." *Narrative Inquiry* 17, no. 1 (2007): 27–47.

Lau, Lisa. "Making the Difference: The Differing Presentations and Representations of South Asia in the Contemporary Fiction of Home and Diasporic South Asian Women Writers." *Modern Asian Studies* 39, no. 1 (2005): 237–56, www.jstor.org/stable/3876512.

Narayan, Uma. *Dislocating Cultures: Identities, Tradition and Third-World*. New York: Routledge, 1997.

Parameswaran, Uma. "Home is Where Your Feet Are, And May Your Heart Be There Too." In *Writers of the Indian Diaspora: Essays on Culture and Identity*, edited by Jasbir Jain, 33–34. Jaipur: Rawat Publications, 2007.

Poddar, Namrata. "'Whiny Assholes' or Creative Hustlers?: On Brownness, Diaspora Fiction, and Western Publication." *Transition*, no. 119 (2016), 92–106.

Rushdie, Salman. *Imaginary Homelands: Essays and Criticism, 1981–1991*. 1st American ed. London: Granta Books, 1991.

Said, Edward. "From *Orientalism.*" In *The Norton Anthology of Theory and Criticism*, edited by Vincent B. Leitch, William E. Cain, Laurie A. Finke, Barbara E. Johnson, John McGowan, and Jeffery J. Williams, 1991–2011. New York, London: W.W. Norton & Company, 2001.

Sen, Amartya. "Indian Traditions and the Western Imagination." *Daedalus* 126, no. 2 (Spring 1997): 1–26.

Syal, Meera. *Life Isn't All Ha Ha Hee Hee*. London: Anchor 2000.

Balli Kaur Jaswal's novels include *The Unlikely Adventures of the Shergill Sisters* and *Erotic Stories for Punjabi Widows*, which was a Reese Witherspoon's Book Club pick in 2018. Born in Singapore and raised in Japan, Russia and the Philippines, Jaswal studied creative writing in the United States and worked as an English teacher in Australia and Turkey. She has held fellowships at the University of East Anglia and Nanyang Technological University, where she also completed her PhD in South Asian diaspora writing. Jaswal's non-fiction has appeared in the *New York Times, Harper's Bazaar India*, Refinery29 and Salon.com, among other publications.

Questions of Race and Audience for BIPOC Writers

David Mura

My evolution as a writer and a person has been intricately involved with my evolving understanding of race in my personal life, in my family, in my community, and in literature and society. I am a third-generation Japanese American. Both my parents' families were imprisoned by the U.S. government during World War II because of their race and ethnicity. My parents were 11 and 15 at the time, and they obviously had committed no act of espionage or treason (no Japanese American was ever convicted of such), so their crime was their race and ethnicity. Both consciously and unconsciously, they responded to their imprisonment by trying to jettison their links to their ethnicity and to become, as much as possible, like white middle-class Americans. Now this is often the tendency of the children of immigrants, but my parents had been imprisoned because they were regarded as aliens, as foreigners and thus, a threat to the nation. As a result, they raised me to be regarded as white and I took it as a compliment when a white friend would say, "I think of you David just like a white person." I was very firmly a so-called banana.

It wasn't until my late twenties, in a profound depression and in therapy, that I happened to pick up Frantz Fanon's *Black Skin, White Masks*. Fanon helped me to finally see my own internalized racism and self-hatred. I began

David Mura
Core Faculty, VONA (Voices of Our Nations
Arts Foundation), Minneapolis, MN, USA

© The Author(s), under exclusive license to Springer Nature Switzerland AG 2022
P. Kaldas, *Writing the Multicultural Experience*,
https://doi.org/10.1007/978-3-031-06124-0_16

reading Black authors and found a language for talking about race that I had not found in any of the white writers I had read in my English Ph.D. program (which I had left with seven incompletes; as I tell my students, I *know* about writers' block). My reading branched out then into writings by Asian Americans and other people of color (POC). At the same time, I was also reading Marxists like Fredric Jameson and Jon Berger, structuralists like Roland Barthes and Foucault, feminists like Adrienne Rich and Susan Griffin, and these writers also taught me to contextualize the individual life within a societal and historical context, how to analyze and deconstruct the reigning ideology of any particular group or historical moment. Later came Said and post-colonial studies, which I discovered in part through teaching a course on post-colonial literature in English. I then went to Japan and writing about that experience in *Turning Japanese* led me to examine how my parents' internment had shaped their own views on race and identity.

All that, though, was easier than what followed. As an arts activist, I helped start an Asian American arts organization and worked with other Asian Americans in the protest of Miss Saigon in the early 1990s. This led me to arguments with white friends about yellow-face casting and the Orientalism in that work, and then, when I wrote about these arguments in *Mother Jones*, I was essentially expelled from the Twin Cities white writing community. At the same time, I was working with the African American writer Alexs Pate on a performance piece about the events in LA surrounding the Rodney King beating and Asian American-African American relations; in constructing that show, we went through intense dialogues and arguments which formed the bond of a permanent friendship between us. I was also making friends with other writers of color and learning from them and their communities. A little later, I wrote a book of poetry, *Colors of Desire*, and a memoir, *Where the Body Meets Memory*, which explored race and sexuality through the lens of my Asian American identity, and this engendered a negative response from certain portions of the Asian American community.

For several years, then, I felt as if both the white writing community and my own community had turned their backs on my work, and I wondered if I had any audience at all. At a certain point, though, I realized that I was who I was, I was writing as truthfully and accurately as I could, and I had to continue exploring my themes and obsessions, no matter the negative responses. It took about five or more years before certain Asian American critics began to write about my work with an understanding of what I was doing rather than a knee-jerk, "he's making us look bad" reaction.

And then I began teaching at VONA, a writers' conference for BIPOC writers taught by BIPOC writers. Amidst the faculty and students at VONA,

I found that I had entered a community that could value my work and who I am and yet who kept challenging me to learn more, to open myself to more of the world. In my teaching at VONA and the Loft literary center, I've had colleagues and students from all over the globe and with many different backgrounds; with many, their lives and families do not fit neatly into certain racial and ethnic boxes or communities.

Similarly, when I arrived in the Twin Cities several decades ago, there was a majority white population and a minority black population, but now over 70 percent of the students are of color, and there are over 130 first languages in the schools. My children grew up in this increasing diversity, and I've learned from them and their friends and from the young people I've worked with here as a writer, a teacher, an activist, and even as a basketball coach. I am constantly made aware of my own ignorance and the limitations of what I know about the world. But that is part of what I love about being a writer. Your subject is the world, and your job is to learn about the world, and that learning should never stop.

In *Pedagogy of the Oppressed*, the great Brazilian educator Paulo Freire states that the oppressed need two languages: First, they need a language to speak about and describe their everyday experiences, what goes on at their work, at home, on the street, in their encounters with others. Second, they need a language to describe how their individual fits in with the workings of the greater society, the structures of power, of the economy, of politics, of culture. Freire argued that if the oppressed do not possess these two languages, they cannot describe their lives and they cannot describe the barriers to their lives, and if they cannot describe the barriers to their lives, they cannot begin to formulate ways of overcoming those barriers and their oppression.

It's obvious that the first language Freire describes is aligned with what we commonly think of as literature, which is also an attempt to describe our everyday lives. But I would argue that the second language, the language which describes the social structures of power is also necessary for writers to acquire; otherwise, their descriptions of their world will lack a necessary component for understanding that world.

More specifically, you cannot begin to describe the U.S., either its past, present, or future, without a language to describe and account for the ways race has shaped this country and continues to shape this country. This means you must understand the history of race in this country; you must understand how our concepts of racial identity were formed and why; you must understand how using the lens of race is essential to understanding what is happening now in this country.

And beyond the social, you must understand how the history of race has formed who you are and how you formulate your own racial identity. This is true for both writers of color and white writers, for we all possess racial identities, both in the ways we think of ourselves and in the ways our society deals with us.

You can't acquire this language being unconscious about your racial identity; nor can you acquire this language without considerable study. Yes, our experience as people of color often provides us with a certain portion of this language; we may obtain some of it from our families or communities and certainly from our literature. But there has been a vast amount of research, both concrete and theoretical, in the area of race in the past few decades, which writers should be acquainted with (e.g., *The New Jim Crow* or *Stamped from the Beginning*); moreover, I believe certain works are absolutely essential to the education of any writer—Fanon's *Black Skin White Masks*, the essays of bell hooks and James Baldwin, Toni Morrison's *Playing in the Dark*, Edward Said's *Culture and Imperialism*, Gates's *Signifying Monkey*, Jeff Chang's *Who We Be*.

I remember running into a young Asian American writer a few years ago who said she didn't want to racially identify her characters. I said that was certainly a literary option. But I then asked her if she had read any of the above works, and she hadn't. So, I told her, "Your aesthetic choices have been shaped only by white writers, by listening to one side of the argument. You aren't making informed choices; you're making the choices your white writing instructors and their ignorance have made for you."

Now in recent years, some of this has begun to change. There are more and more writers and readers of color, and we are growing at a faster rate than the white population. Moreover, more writers of color are taking creative writing classes, getting MFA's and/or taking advantage of avenues to study writing and literature with other writers of color. The VONA writers' conference for writers of color—which I have taught at for almost twenty years—is part of this, so are Cave Canem, Kundiman, Macondo, and others. Then too when a writer from one community really breaks through, such as has occurred with Toni Morrison or Louise Erdrich or Maxine Hong Kingston or Viet Thanh Nguyen, that creates openings for other writers from the same community. And of course, we learn from each other; my guess is that Tommy Orange learned a lot from Louise Erdrich, but perhaps he also learned from the short stories of Junot Diaz and from *The Brief Wondrous History of Oscar Wao* (just as I learned from Morrison and Maxine Hong Kingston's memoirs). Part of what Orange might have learned is that he could write out of his own experience and out of his own community and he didn't have to make any of that particularly palatable or understandable to a white middleclass reader.

In the introduction to *A Stranger's Journey*, I quote from Jeff Chang's *Who We Be: The Colorization of America*. Chang examines the issues of race over the last fifty years, the post-civil rights era, within the context of cultural change. The book explores moments like Black Arts Movement, the advent of multi-culturalism, and the so-called culture wars:

> Here is where artists and those who work and play in the culture enter. They help people to see what cannot yet be seen, hear the unheard, tell the untold. They make change feel not just possible, but inevitable. Every moment of major social change requires a collective leap of imagination. Change presents itself not only in spontaneous and organized expressions of unrest and risk, but in explosions of mass creativity.
>
> So those interested in transforming society might assert: cultural change always precedes political change. Put another way, political change is the last manifestation of cultural shifts that have already occurred.

As everyone now knows, sometime around 2040 or sooner, we will no longer be a white majority country. No racial group will constitute the majority. Artists of color, who are recreating the past, exploring our present, and creating our future, know what it means to be a racial minority in America. White artists and white America generally lack this knowledge.

We are in the midst of a crisis right now over who is an American and thus what America has been, is now, and will be in the future. Writers of color are essential to understanding the causes and nature of this crisis, and they are certainly more and more essential to the portrait of who we are as a country.

But we have a long way to go; there are so many ways that writers of color are still marginalized in the literary world—especially in terms of reviews, publishing, and the ways creative writing is taught. My recent book, *A Stranger's Journey: Race, Identity & Narrative Craft in Writing*, presents creative, aesthetic, and political arguments why the issues of race and identity should be a standard part of teaching creative writing. Certainly, the white writing world still needs a great deal of education to properly contextualize and evaluate our work.

In the book, I have an essay "The Student of Color in the Typical MFA Program," and I continue to get e-mails from students of color in MFA programs who tell me that the events I describe in the essay are happening to them—the refusal of white students and white instructors to deal with the issues of race in writing; the various dumb and/or racist readings of the student of color's work or the appearance of stereotypes and one-dimensional characters of color in the work of white students; the casting of the student of color's critiques as either a personal problem of their individual character or attempts at censorship or the enforcement of PC rules in writing. As I point out, these arguments are both aesthetic and political; they are arguments between groups, not simply involving the individuals in the classroom. That is why these arguments occur in classes all over the country: The push back against race and racial issues in literature is not, at its heart, very different from the push back against race and racial issues in any other area of society or institution.

As an example of how a writing workshop designed for BIPOC writers can help us involves the question of audience—whom does one write for? I often tell my students of color: You don't have to write for the dumbest, most igno- rant racist reader. So don't spend a lot of time thinking about how that dumb and ignorant reader is going to misread your work. Don't spend a lot of time fearing or trying to answer stupid and uninformed critiques of your work.

Conversely, there are still many white writers who don't think about how readers of color might critique their work. That is one reason why so many white writers remain unconscious of the racial implications of their work or what a racial reading of their work might reveal.

In *Playing in the Dark; Whiteness and The Literary Imagination,* Toni Morrison gets at these concerns when she asks: "What happens to the writerly imagination of a Black author who is at some level *always* conscious of repre- senting one's own race to, or in spite of, a race of readers that understands itself to be "universal" or race-free?" As Morrison points out, her dangers are not in resorting to the tropes white writers have used to construct "literary blackness":

> Neither blackness nor "people of color" stimulates in me notions of excessive, limitless love, anarchy, or routine dread. I cannot rely on these metaphorical shortcuts because I am a black writer struggling with and through a language that can powerfully evoke and enforce hidden signs of racial superiority, cultural hegemony, and dismissive "othering" of people and language which are by no means marginal or already and completely known and knowable in my work. My vulnerability would lie in romanticizing blackness rather than demonizing it; vilifying whiteness rather than reifying it. The kind of work I have always wanted to do requires me to learn how to maneuver ways to free up the language from its sometimes sinister, frequently lazy, almost always predictable employ- ment of racially informed and determined chains.

Morrison implies that an informed Black reader or writer would be better able to point out where she is "exoticizing," to use your question's term, than your average white reader or writer. But of course, her remarks also imply that other Black writers may also be guilty of using lazy or exoticizing language. Certainly, we've all been at readings, especially poetry readings, where we're confronted with what is more agitprop than literature or where we're hearing the ethnic food poem that we've all heard before.

In *A Stranger's Journey*, in my essay on the four questions regarding the narrator, I suggest that one way of confronting these problems involves the question: "Whom is the narrator telling the tale to?" You can, for instance, picture your narrator telling the tale to your average white audience and explaining everything that the audience would be ignorant of or not be able to contextualize. This is basically the strategy of Aravind Adiga's *The White Tiger* where the narrator, a Bangalore businessman who grew up in a poor village, is writing a letter to the Premier of China and thus explains everything in India that the Chinese premier would not understand or know about. But there is also the option to tell the tale to members of your own community, as Junot Diaz does in *The Brief Wondrous History of Oscar Wao*; that audience would not be interested in self-exoticizing their own experience or the protagonist's or the author's.

In an interview, one of my former students asked about the question of exoticizing your material as a BIPOC writer, and this essay is an answer to that student. I told him: You don't have to write for the white reader; you can write for readers for your own community, and why would you exoticize yourself to your own community?

I would also suggest that exoticizing arises in part out of a desire, perhaps unconscious on the writer's part, to avoid more difficult and painful areas of the writer's experience or more conflicted aspects of the writer's community or family. In other words, exoticizing can arise when the writer is focusing on the surface of their experience, rather than the complicated and often painful depths; in other words, you as a writer should be lasering in on what has been repressed or denied as opposed to the tropes, images, and stories that may be more readily available and consumed. Dig deeper, be more honest, and don't write away from your fears or pain or complications but into them.

Acknowledgment This essay was based on an interview originally published in *Hyphen-Asian American Unabridged*, Jan 17, 2019. [author retains copyright]

David Mura is a poet, creative nonfiction and fiction writer, critic, playwright and performance artist. Mura's latest book is on creative writing and race, *A Stranger's Journey: Race, Identity & Narrative Craft in Writing* (2018). A Sansei or third generation Japanese American, Mura has written two memoirs: *Turning Japanese: Memoirs of a Sansei*, which won a 1991 Josephine Miles Book Award from the Oakland PEN and was listed in the New York Times Notable Books of Year, and *Where the Body Meets Memory: An Odyssey of Race, Sexuality and Identity* (1996). With essayist Carolyn Holbrook, Mura is co-editor of an anthology of Minnesota BIPOC writers, *We Are Meant to Rise: Voices for Justice from Minneapolis to the World*, to be published in Nov. 2021. His next book is *The Stories Whiteness Tells Itself*, a collection of essays contrasting historical and fiction narratives by white Americans and African Americans, appearing in fall 2022.

The Eternal Gain That Is Translation

Khaled Mattawa

You all know the expression "lost in translation." While there is a grain of truth in this adage, its absolute opposite is much more true. Without translation, the English language would not have gained the King James Bible. Without translation, Shakespeare would not have heard of Othello and many of the other subjects of his plays. Without translation, we would not have had the sonnet (from the Italian sonnet); we would not have had Donne, Herbert, or Marvel. Clearly, we gain a great deal from translation.

As a conceptual practice, translation takes place in many of our daily activities. Let me give this analogy. Let's say there's a building in another country that we would like to build a replica of in our city. Once we've found the blueprints of the original, we will have to start "translating" them into concrete, brick, wood, mortar, steel, and glass, or whatever our local materials may be. A few lines on a piece of paper do not in themselves make a wall or a window. It takes an engineer to know what they refer to in terms of size, thickness, and exact placing. And this person must check and recheck the blueprint to make sure he has the design right. If he doesn't understand what a symbol means, he must check his manuals and consult with experts and other builders who've encountered similar problems. If he cannot find certain materials indicated in the blueprint, he will have to see about finding equivalent materials that would render the original intent. In this case, the builder,

K. Mattawa
University of Michigan, Ann Arbor, MI, USA
e-mail: kmattawa@umich.edu

P. Kaldas, *Writing the Multicultural Experience*,
https://doi.org/10.1007/978-3-031-06124-0_17

167

like a translator, must attempt to be faithful to the original plan and creative in putting the building together.

And as in every act of creativity, bad execution will mar a brilliant idea. A painter with great ideas will fail to "translate" them into paintings or sculptures if he has little command of technique. The freshest and most wholesome fruits and vegetables, the best cuts of meat, and the most exquisite herbs and spices do not in themselves make a great meal; it takes a skillful cook to assemble them together.

What are the necessary skills of a translator? She or he must have mastery in reading the language of the original text and mastery in writing in the host language. Translation experts have argued through the ages as to which is more important. I think both skills are essential. A good poet in his own language with weak command of the original language is likely to translate a poem in very readable fashion, but that it may have glaring errors. What about a person with excellent command of the original language but with poor poetic skills in the host language? Here we should expect a very accurate, literal poem, but that gives us no pleasure because it lacks other forms of precision that we expected in our language. Many translations are collaborative projects between a scholar of the original language and a poet skilled in the poetic techniques of his own language.

Translation, even of literature, does not take place in a political and economic vacuum. When we read a translated poem, we unconsciously bring with us assumptions about the culture where the original poem comes from. This happens to translators as well. As an attempt to experience another culture, translation has to contend with such unconscious assumptions. And as in any dialogue, if you're not listening to what a person is saying, you are likely to assume something based on what you already think of that person. To translate means you have to pay attention to everything being said, and you have to understand why it is being said the way it is being said. And then you do your best to paraphrase what you heard keeping all the nuances intact.

A few years ago, I likened translation to ballroom dancing. For the dance to succeed, both dancers must pay attention to what the other is doing. Yet while they move jointly, each dancer is moving independently and is responding to his or her own impulses. A translator's job is to create a partner to the original text that matches it, but is skillful on its own. In my translations of Arabic poetry, I try to create various renditions of the poem. In my lap, I always have an English dictionary, an Arabic dictionary, and an English thesaurus at hand. If I still don't understand a word or a line, I ask the poet, if he or she is available to me. I check with scholars of Arabic and have them go through my renditions. And finally, I show it to poets who don't know the original language to see if the poem is coherent in English and if it has a musical quality. I leave the poem alone for a few days or weeks, and go over it again, and again, until I feel I have satisfied both my concerns about accuracy and about the quality of the result.

Translated poems tend to sound slightly unfamiliar but are imbued with an inner logic. In a sense, that is what other cultures are like. I avoid American English colloquialisms in translation and allow the images and the metaphors of the original language to present the ideas of the poem. Some poems refuse translations; they possess linguistic qualities and word play that are unique to Arabic that would require a great deal of explanation, beyond what a translator can do, to render them correctly. Some things are like that: plants that would not grow outside their native soil or climate. A simplistic or unskillful attempt at translating them may rob them of the originality and brilliance they possess in their original language.

So as a translator one has to accept such limitations. And in fact, one grows to enjoy the uniquenesses of other languages and other cultures through encountering these difficulties as much as through succeeding in rendering a foreign poem into English. It means we have to try harder to expand our language and our thinking to welcome such different notions. I once heard an Italian professor say, that since the collapse of the mythical tower of Babel, "the only language of God is the language of translation." It is a process that requires fidelity, devotion, open-mindedness, and creativity. That's how we speak to God, and that is how he speaks to us. And that is too how we should speak to each other, through empathy and attention. An act of translation abiding by these principles can only be a gain, not a loss, to us.

Acknowledgment The essay was originally published in *Poetry International* [All rights to the work reverted to the author upon publication.]

Khaled Mattawa is the author of five books of poetry, most recently *Fugitive Atlas* (Graywolf 2020). He is also the author of *Mahmoud Darwish: The Poet's Art and His Nation*, a critical study of the great Palestinian poet Mahmoud Darwish, and *How Long Have You Been with Us: Essays on Poetry*. Mattawa has translated numerous books of contemporary Arabic poetry and co-edited three anthologies of Arab American literature. A MacArthur Fellow, Mattawa teaches at the University of Michigan and edits *Michigan Quarterly Review*.

Loosening the Collars

Rebecca Balcárcel

Students file in with a quiet swish of leggings and jeans. For most, this is their first college class; their nervousness charges the air. A few have returned from military duty, wage work, or parenting, rounding the curve of their twenties, hoping to fuel up for their next stage. Some have put off this English class until last, dreading the essays and research paper, certain their words will continually dart out of reach, never be lured to the page. Others think writing means typing out fringe-dripping sentences until the word count is reached.

All come with collars.

As they say their names and also one quote, song lyric, or book they love, I start to see what kinds of collars I'm dealing with. Latavia's is tight, but lime green and sequined. She uses her "white girl" voice, as she'll call it later, to perfectly annunciate to us that her favorite book is *The Things They Carried*. Reneé pulls at his red leather collar as he explains that he has never finished a book, but he likes the Golden Rule. Jolie tells us their favorite song is the soundtrack to a video game whose name I don't catch.

I let go the stipulation that my icebreaker instructions call for a lyric, because I see that Jolie's collar is a lot like mine. Fraying, looser than in years past, but stubbornly stiff, almost sailcloth weight, and purple.

Papers, they will write. Articles and essays, they will read. Speeches and argumentation, they will analyze. But my real course goal is to stretch the collars, to let loose every voice.

R. Balcárcel
Tarrant County College, FortWorth, TX, USA

I didn't notice my own collar until graduate school. I started my MFA after years of dutifully writing poems that imitated canon authors and contemporary poets of the U.S. And why not? I deeply appreciated—indeed, appreciate now—their word play, their precision, their earned truths. I didn't know the word "colonized" as we use it today. I only knew that great writers of English had touched me, and I wanted to touch readers in my turn.

I ignored the fact that my father, half my DNA and half of my personal world, wasn't from the U.S., the U.K., or even one of the many places where the British Empire poured its language over the land like a thick porridge. For me, it only mattered that moments of buoyant insight and wet eyes looking up from a printed page were destinations reached by English roads.

And yet.

Wasn't it true that I'd been rocked to sleep with Spanish lullabies? Hadn't my father's eyes teared up after the ring of a guitar chord and the final, rhyming line of a bolero? Didn't he quote Cervantes and Lorca and the romantic, accessible Bécquer, looking into the middle distance and savoring their beauty before turning his amazed eyes on me?

Yes.

And didn't my father's flamboyant metaphors and constant personification—not only was the car a "she," but the deck, the lawnmower, and, tenderly, the guitar—affect my ideas of how language could be used, if one dared?

But I didn't dare.

For years, the collar thickened around my throat, stiffening with the unvoiced, unuttered-even-to-myself conviction that I must write the "right" way. Everything depended upon becoming an expert at that game. And by everything, I meant wide readership, publication, and acceptance into the club of people who announced with confidence that they were writers. After all, every MFA student at my graduate school that first semester was white except me, as far as I could tell. All but one faculty member, too, came from the culture that I didn't think of as merely dominant, but as the one, actual, uniocular reality. What else was there?

One would be forgiven for thinking me dense, or at least naïve. How could I think that half of me was the whole?

It didn't help that, across my childhood, seeing my father's language in action came with cringe. Sure, when we visited my Guatemalan relatives, his stories set the place rocking with laughter, but in other contexts, I picked up a vibe of—well?—condescension? Teenage me had trouble labeling it, but I saw the tilted heads of cashiers and neighbors. I saw their good hearts straining to hear beyond his Spanish accent, their slowly nodding heads trying to follow his thinking. They often smiled or even laughed at the right moments, but with a sense of indulging him, of being polite. A whiff of pity floated from where they stood, their footing firm on a concrete step higher than his, their insider's place assured. When I learned the phrase "prestige language," I understood that Spanish in the U.S. wasn't it.

They weren't smarter, these people, nor did they necessarily think they were. They weren't more familiar with formal English—my dad used "whom" like a perfectly placed note in a symphony. They understood most of his individual words. They liked him. They just didn't get—what was it? A heart-thing I could see my father trying to give them, some context within which the story made more sense, some approach to living that would make his words not thud, but ring. It's hard to quantify, but I could tell that anything my father said to most people would always be slightly out of phase, like a radio station broadcasting on a frequency one tenth of a degree off from their receivers.

To be fair, friends and family gave my father more to work with. More esteem, more time, more effort. He got to know them and vice-versa.

But I saw the disadvantage he was at with strangers. I saw the assumptions they were trying not to make and the extra warmth he added to his smile to pre-empt the effect his accent would have. Even if everyone gave their best to the whole situation, there was a gap. And maybe there's always a gap between humans, between souls; maybe it wasn't all cultural misfire, but I, young and inexperienced, didn't want it. And with my American-born English, I didn't have it. In verbal conversation, if my slight tan and three-syllable last name worried anyone, my English put them at ease. When I turned to writing, especially artistic writing—fiction, poetry—I deployed the same strategy. Write to be accepted. Write to be taken seriously. Write for the presumed audience of book-buyers. Write white.

So "daring" was off-limits.
Enter the collar.

The collar was my idea of what real writing looked like. It was my word-hoard and my iambic drum. It was a red wheelbarrow glazed with Dickensian dashes beside the white, less-traveled chickens. All of which would have been fine if it had been me. All of me.

And here readers may say that they, too, felt the collar tightening when they started writing seriously or when they started writing for tests and college assignments. They, too, held out their hand to receive a baton from Shakespeare, but taking it, stopped in their tracks, unsure of how to pass it on. It's not only brown folks who struggle to find an authentic voice. It's all of us.

Thus, my students come in timid. Hailing from different backgrounds, economic levels, orientations, and cultures, they carry both the fear of and the wish for conformity. They love being individual, but they want to write correctly or at least in a way that pleases me. They guess at what college writing means and keep a tab on their browser open to thesaurus.com.

They also bring in their past. They bring admonitions, such as "Don't use singular 'they'"; they bring the words First, Secondly, Finally; they bring the five-paragraph paper; they bring startling statistics with which to open every essay; they bring APA, MLA, Chicago Style; they bring Show, not Tell; they bring "In conclusion"; they bring the thesis that lists three things; one in twenty bring the Oxford comma; seventeen in twenty bring topic sentences; twenty in twenty bring anxiety and the hope that this class won't tank their grade point average.

> Some of these are useful. (I love the Oxford comma nearly as much as I love my cat.)
> Some are crutches, but better than nothing.
> Some, unneeded.
> All of them, proscriptive.

Which is not all bad. (Another rule: Never open a sentence with "Which" in this way.) Plenty of students appreciate direction and a decent amount of demystification when it comes to writing, but too many, in my experience, have learned to crank out inert pieces that fall flat. Worse, they come to the classroom thinking that writing is a mechanical exercise that has very little to do with their real selves. They haven't thought of putting themselves on the page, nor been encouraged to, except in the narrow frame of taking a position on an issue or policy. When asked to describe their voice, they don't think they have one.

This was me the day I first put the word "Guatemala" in a poem.

I had just read eight packets of my classmates' poems. These were graduate students, so the work was competent, even good. It was so good that I sat back, intimidated. Everyone seemed to be throwing down words like challenges. Not to me, but to the reader. My own packet seemed tame, tentative.

Maybe I was inventing a confidence my classmates didn't really have, but their pages made me restless. Suddenly I was aware of an energy within myself that I'd never tried to put into words. Along with ideas of what vocabulary I "should" use had come ideas of what I "should" write about and what poems "should" look like. Seeing the variety of my classmates' work was a tap on the shoulder. The tap became a shove when I remembered a book that wowed my world, *The House on Mango Street* by Sandra Cisneros. Then a recent discovery in the poetry of Mary Oliver, the prose poem, seemed to yell, *What are you doing? If you're going to be a real poet, you need to go deeper, get real-er, write in a form that takes its shape from the content.*

I opened my spiral notebook and wrote as if in a trance. Writing is often more like laying bricks than waving wands, but once in a decade or so, it happens. I swung open the door separating my two halves. I wrote the most true thing I could: "Guatemala was a place inside my closet." I went on to write a paragraph-long story about the excitement and fear of acknowledging a hidden self. I relished run-on sentences, building cadences that echoed my father's way of circling round and round a point before revealing it. I wove a Whitmanesque excess with the fiesta flavors of celebration—or tried to. I wasn't sure what I was doing, but that was the adventure. I wrote dangerously, improperly, riskily. I pulled from everywhere, mixing mangos and apples, merging the energy streams of a brown girl feeling white and a white-passing girl yessing her brown. When I looked up from the page, I knew my writing would never be the same.

An experience of self and the self's voice—that's what I want my students to reach toward.

That's why I start with the opposite. I open the class with a grandfather collar-maker, Professor Higgins.

Once the students have introduced themselves, I put Professor Higgins on screen. We listen to him sing, "Why Can't the English Teach Their Children How to Speak?" from *My Fair Lady*. He rails against people "down in Soho square, dropping h's everywhere" and frets that "one common language … we'll never get" (Rex Harrison). He asserts that accents alone create a "verbal class distinction." His solution is to make everyone speak the same way—his way, of course. At first, students often agree. And they typically think I do, too.

We talk about standard English and its power; we talk about how academic English is practically a dialect of its own, and I promise to teach it to them.

Then we listen to an opposite view from "trilingual orator" Jamila Lyiscott. She explains that her TED Talk is a "linguistic celebration," because she speaks Jamaican Patois, street English, and formal English. She further explains that saying "Hello" in her neighborhood would be inarticulate because one ought to say, "Wus good?" (Lyiscott).

I put students in groups to examine these and similar questions: (1) Is there such a thing as language profiling? (2) Have you experienced language stereotyping? (3) Are all accents equal? (4) Is there one best way to speak English? (5) What Englishes are you aware of? (6) How much should context determine which language you use?

This is when I see a thawing in the students' manner. A loosening of the collars. They're starting to get the (correct) idea that they might be able to bring their whole self to this classroom and even to their writing.

At this point, I often recommend they take the New York Times Dialect Quiz, an online questionnaire that predicts where users grew up based on their answers. We sometimes work through it as a class and laugh about who says lightning bug versus firefly, who says pop versus soda versus Coke, and who pronounces pajamas with an ah in the second syllable.

Their homework is to tell the same incident in two voices, making sure that one uses slang or code-switching or words I won't know.

By the end of day one, they see that I'm more interested in them developing their voices than in them learning mine. I do teach them "academic speak," but only after honoring their many ways of communicating. Their first big paper is about language itself, a variation on the literacy narrative. Multilingual students have a lot to say, and my Texas natives often explore how they are keeping or not keeping their Southern drawl and why. Some students talk about translation or code-switching; others examine their in-group talk, memes, or family idioms.

Not every student makes a breakthrough, of course, but almost all of them see each other in a new light. To share one's language is to share one's identity. Through class discussion and the exchange of essays, every student becomes more fully human to their classmates.

They all walk in, as I did to class after class, with an expectation that they'll need to hide parts of themselves, de-emphasize their differences, sound like generic college students, dim their light. Hopefully, they leave with the opposite idea: that being their full selves is the best route to effective writing.

Works Cited

Lyiscott, Jamila. "3 Ways to Speak English." *Jamila Lyiscott: 3 Ways to Speak English | TED Talk*, https://www.ted.com/talks/jamila_lyiscott_3_ways_to_speak_english?language=en.

Rex Harrison. *Why Can't the English*. YouTube. https://www.youtube.com/watch?v=KftTPpWdcCM.

Rebecca Balcárcel loves teaching her students at Tarrant County College as Associate Professor of English and writing bi-cultural stories. Her novels are *Shine On, Luz Véliz!*, and *The Other Half of Happy*, which was named a Pura Belpré Honor Book, an ALSC Notable Book, and an Américas Award silver medalist. Her next book is *Bridges and Islands: 20 Stories by Multiracial and Multicultural Authors* for which she is both co-editor and contributor. Find Rebecca at rebeccabalcarcel.com, on Twitter as @r_balcarcel, and on YouTube where she analyzes literature and chats about writing as the SixMinuteScholar.

A Mapmaker's Journey

Lisa Suhair Majaj

My writing has been a navigation across uncertain terrain: a mapmaker's journey through conflicting geographies. The terrain is in part literal: from the
small farming community of Hawarden, Iowa, where I was born and to which
I returned throughout my childhood; to the California landscape where my
parents tried and failed to find a foothold when I was an infant; to Beirut, a
way-stop of employment for my father in his attempt to get closer to home;
to the stony hills of Amman, Jordan, where we settled in a small stone house
shortly before my fourth birthday, joining my father's exiled Palestinian family; to Iowa, where my mother and sister and I fled during Jordan's civil war in
1970, Black September, before returning to Jordan the following summer; to
Massachusetts, where I completed my last year of high school at a boarding
school that offered me a scholarship when I could not find an English school
in Jordan; to Lebanon again, where I studied at the American University of
Beirut in the middle of the civil war, met the Greek Cypriot who was to
become my life partner, Andreas Alexandrou, evacuated out in the middle of
the 1982 Israeli invasion on a cargo ship, and was hijacked by the Israeli navy
and taken to Haifa for interrogation; to Michigan, where I went to graduate
school and gained the tools to explore my identity as an Arab American, and
where I met Pauline Kaldas, my lifelong friend, without whose encouragement I might never have found the courage to write seriously; to Massachusetts

L. S. Majaj
Nicosia, Cyprus

© The Author(s), under exclusive license to Springer Nature Switzerland AG 2022
P. Kaldas, *Writing the Multicultural Experience*,
https://doi.org/10.1007/978-3-031-06124-0_19

again, where I deepened my community consciousness and activist commitment as an Arab American; and then in 2001 to the dusty brown and shimmering blue space of Cyprus, the island where I created a new home, raised my children, lost my husband after a long struggle with cancer, and now find myself once again struggling to remake myself.

The terrain is also non-literal: an internal landscape of complexity and multiplicity, experience and emotion, across which I travel searching for identity, belonging, a way forward. Within this landscape, strands of perception and memory and questioning interweave to construct a reality always in process, never entirely resolved: woven, unwoven, rewoven, like the braid my mother plaited for me daily, crisscrossing the strands, each time with a slightly different pressure; sometimes pulled tight, hurting my scalp, other times smoothed softly, or interlaced in a rush, so that wisps fell into my eyes, blurring my vision. So many ways to tangle and untangle; so many ways in which to be lost, to be found or find oneself, to succumb to confusion, create order, navigate displacement and loss and love, move from chaos to calm to creation, silence to voice.

My writing emerges from this weaving and reweaving of multiple strands; from the vulnerability of moving through conflicting, intertwined worlds fraught with risk. It emerges from the need to understand myself and the spaces I have inhabited, left behind, claimed. As a child, I had no tools to process the confusions of my life. Though from a young age I had already traveled far, changed continents, crossed oceans, the journey to myself was another matter. My parents were each, in different ways, exiled: my mother from the U.S., my father from Palestine. As for me, I was an exile from myself, navigating the language of bifurcation: half this, half that, always out of place. I had not yet found the hyphen to join my broken parts, much less the tools to interrogate it. I did not know how to say I was Arab American, Palestinian American: a whole.

But I learned early that using language in a conscious way offered a sense of control over uncertainty as well as a way to challenge the constraints that bound me. When I was in first or second grade, I published my first poems in the school magazine, *The Square Circle*, small stanzas whose creation I now understand offered me both a structure and an opening. How perfect that name was for a magazine of writing by third culture and hybrid children, residents of an in-between zone in which reality never quite fit into the boxes of cultural expectations, in which we were, indeed, constantly trying to square the circle. With the help of inspiring teachers, especially Sue Dahdah and Diana Saleh, I learned that writing opened doors both inward and outwards. In this way, writing became part of my journey toward myself. I learned that a poem opens a space in both the reader and the writer, a space into which many things can enter. The distance between those first poems and today is a lifetime; the words mapping that distance served as a lifeline. When I started researching Arab American literature, I learned even more clearly how literature is a map: reading it we find our way, writing it we map the path for others as well as for ourselves.

To write is to engage in a risky act. It requires both looking inward and speaking out: both may seem dangerous or impossible. How much more difficult when the self from which one writes is a jumbled terrain without signposts? I was silenced by both internal and external factors—the trauma of displacement and war (as a child I lived through the 1967 war, 1970 Black September, the 1973 war); family confusions and cultural injunctions; feelings of inadequacy (I recall in particular a professor who told me to read "everything" before daring to write anything); and my growing understanding that while writing about Palestine was risky business, voicing internal cultural critique was a kind of community betrayal. Writer's block, my longtime companion, was one result of that layered silencing. But in understanding that my words could both express the self and respond to the world, I discovered the dual gesture of language: at once the most private form of expression, and the most public. I learned that what is needed are both words and a space in which words can be spoken and heard.

I found my writer's voice at this intersection of personal and political. In 1987, I was researching and writing about Arab American literature and becoming more involved with Palestinian activism and dialogue. Then the first Intifada began in Palestine, and a few months later my Palestinian father died. I found myself grappling with my personal connection to familial loss while at the same time responding to political events and Palestine on an acutely visceral level. I turned to poetry to process and articulate the emotions I was experiencing and to speak out against the violence I was witnessing. Writing gave me a way to respond to the urgency of the news, to make a space for Palestinian identity, to locate myself and to speak from that location. This was not an easy thing: there was scant space for Palestinian voices in the U.S. at the time. But poetry helped me find space in a wider sphere: it allowed me to speak for myself and for others, as part of a larger whole.

My writing process similarly emerges from the urgency of my subject matter, the pressure of internal emotion, and the need to speak out on both a personal and public level. Working my way through complexity, I confront distances, erasures, and urgencies. The page opens a path in me: following it, I find a path to both myself and the world. Much of my writing is intuitive; I follow the perception, the emotion, the line to where it takes me. I typically begin with free writing—in response to a news item, an image, a phrase, a sound, a memory, or simply the moment where pen meets paper or fingers meet keyboard. I try to write quickly, to catch the end of the linguistic thread, and to follow where it leads. In this way, I succumb to forces larger than me, to the urgency within and without, allowing my subconscious to make connections and intersections—drawing on experience, perception, intellect, memory, sensory experience, history, politics, and more.

The writing process then shifts from internal landscapes to the text itself. My approach to craft is a mixture of moving by feel and conscious literary technique. What form the poem takes is sometimes inherent from the beginning; at other times, it emerges as I work with the language, using linguistic structures to help bring out the internal core of the piece. For instance, one early published poem, "Claims," uses anaphora to frame a series of claims about my identity—*I am, I am not.* The poem came out of my need to assert identity and reality against the societal denial and erasure of Palestinians—to push away imposed definitions and stereotypes and assert a voice, claim space for being. The urgency of this need to assert identity was operative on both a personal and a political level, and informed the poem's format and rhetorical choices.

Working with poetic elements such as line length, line breaks, and stanza form offers a way to engage with the emotion of the poem, not just shaping and controlling it, but also allowing its internal energy to reveal itself. My poems tend to go through multiple drafts, in which each change creates ripple effects. Experimenting with line breaks leads to shifts in language, as I search for words with the exact cadence or syllabic length or consonant sound or fluidity or abruptness necessary for the shape and body and musculature of a particular line. These shifts allow the layers of meaning to deepen. Experimentation with different stanza forms—couplets, triplets, tercets, free verse—similarly leads the poem through transformations, deletions, compressions, expansions. Each variation allows something slightly different to be highlighted, providing a way to channel the emotional and perceptual and intellectual core of the poem; seeing what comes to the foreground through this experimentation guides my choices. Every line or stanza of poetry exists both in its language and in the shape of the language on the page; I have learned that working with white space creates the potential for layers to deepen. This literary process is, by and large, visceral, yet is guided by an intellectual awareness of how poetic language and form come together to create meaning.

While I often start with a chunk of free-form prose that I transform into a poem through line breaks, stanzas, and fine-tuning of language and structure, sometimes it's the reverse: when a poem won't come together in any of the forms I've tried, I put it into a block of text to see what happens—sometimes a poem needs that rush of language without end stops or white space for its internal voice to emerge. Or I allow fragments of text—words or phrases—to move across the page, allowing the white space between them, the staggering of lines and phrases across the page, to contribute to the work of creating meaning. I also on occasion work with traditional forms. In a kind of opposition to harnessing a rush of language whose current is elusive, imposing a formal linguistic structure from the beginning with strict requirements of line length, repetition, and so on can lead to unexpected discoveries of both language and meaning.

Most of the imagery in my poems comes out of memory and sensory experience although images may migrate across locations or exist in multiple locations—for example, bougainvillea in Jordan, Palestine, Cyprus; the brilliance of fall leaves in the U.S. echoing spring blossoms in Lebanon. Images are like sparks in my mind; they light small fires and often flare unbidden. Sometimes a poem requires the juxtaposition of different locations, and this interplay between locations, like the interplay between past and present, is not reducible to a linearity: the past is not always past, the present is not always resolved. In addition, there are structures of power and structures of violence and structures of loss situating these poems. Imagery exists not just as beauty but as piecing illumination into what exists, what is lost, what is destroyed, what persists, what is remembered, what can be imagined or brought into being or changed. The human consciousness experiencing these geographies is both witness and participant; the "I" of the poem bears a responsibility as well as a visceral need to remember, to speak.

I write out of a belief that poetry's ability to convey what one interlocutor termed "the interior emotional landscape of individual experience" can somehow make a shift—if not in the world, then in individuals, who may then go on to do things in the world that make a difference. It is true that words too often seem futile in the face of oppression. But words are a form of resistance. They take a stand in the world. Written firstly for the poet, they address readers in a multitude of ways. They invite, they evoke, they plead, they exhort. They touch readers, and that process of touching is an opening.

I have been deeply shaped by so many writers. When I first came to the U.S., Maxine Hong Kingston's memoir, *The Woman Warrior*, modeled the possibility of writing personally about the convoluted web of ethnic heritage, while Joy Harjo's poetry offered an intense poetic language, voicing urgent histories. These and other writers of different ethnic and native backgrounds inspired me to discover the literature of Arab Americans—and to begin writing myself. But it is my personal friendships with Arab American writers, many of whom I found while researching the still nascent body of Arab American literature, that has been the most deeply formative influence on my writing life. My long-term friendship with Pauline Kaldas has been especially significant: she encouraged my writing, responded to my work, and heard the deep core of what I was trying to say. I have learned so much from her poetic voice and insight. I have been inspired by her in countless ways, and am deeply grateful for her companionship in our Arab American journey. Naomi Shihab Nye played a similarly important role for my life and work. I first found her writing while researching Arab American writing for my PhD; a poetry workshop I took with her later initiated an ongoing friendship. In her words and her presence, I have felt the pieces of my life, my work, and my Palestinian American identity come together. From her, I learned the value of seeing the world in different ways and representing it through different literary forms: it is because of her that I wrote my first children's book. I am also deeply grateful to Mohja Kahf for her writing and energy and inspiration. My comments about poetic technique in this essay were first drafted in response to her students, with whom I had an invigorating online interchange.

And I am filled with gratitude to so many other Arab American writers and scholars who have helped map the journey, find the path, and chart the opening possibilities before us. *Alf shukran*. We walk this road together.

Lisa Suhair Majaj is the author of *Geographies of Light* (poetry, 2009) and other creative work and critical work. She co-edited *Intersections: Gender, Nation and Community in Arab Women's Novels* (2002), *Etel Adnan: Critical Essays on the Arab-American Writer and Artist* (2002) and *Going Global: The Transnational Reception of Third World Women Writers* (2000), and has written extensively about Arab-American literature. Widely published internationally, she has read at many international events. Her poetry was displayed in the photography exhibition Aftermath: The Fallout of War—America and the Middle East (Harn Museum of Art, 2016).

Call and Response: Writing Lives

T. J. Anderson III

You're probably at the point where you are trying to figure out the value of writing, and maybe, if you're in a class, you're also wondering why you even need any sort of "instruction." More specifically, you may be having some concerns about your writing and why you do it. Maybe you're concerned about what you imagine for it. Perhaps you spend an inordinate amount of time contemplating your identity as a "writer of color." How did the predicament of Western history and identity politics get you to this place? Be assured that you are not the first to have such thoughts. Read Langston Hughes's "The Negro Artist and the Racial Mountain" to understand how the issue of identity is crucial to the artist's connection with their community. And while it is fine to ruminate over such questions, it's important to remember that "thinking" about writing is not writing itself. While thinking can be a prelude to writing, it can also be seen as a kind of luxury because it offers the illusion of choice. Given the history of white supremacy in this country, I feel I have very little time to ruminate on my position of writer as that is one of witness during rapidly changing times that continue to aspire toward my silencing. I have the responsibility to, like my dad says, "document the culture," and it's crucial that I make writing my practice, put my voice on the page, and share it with the community.

I don't know if you're the kind of writer who feels like there is nothing else you want to do but write and you'll go to great extremes if you can't. Without

T. J. Anderson III
Hollins University, Roanoke, VA, USA
e-mail: tanderson@hollins.edu

© The Author(s), under exclusive license to Springer Nature Switzerland AG 2022
P. Kaldas, *Writing the Multicultural Experience*,
https://doi.org/10.1007/978-3-031-06124-0_20

185

doubt, there is an intensity to that kind of calling. Perhaps more, this idea is further affirmed when people say you had a relative or an ancestor who had similar talents and aspirations. Maybe you were the kind of person who devoured books under the dark covers of your bed. Perhaps you found yourself experiencing the wealth of knowledge in a library. I think this speaks to a particular kind of passion. If you are of this group, consider yourself fortunate. Yes, I'm sure everyone can relay stories of their literary ancestors who went to great lengths to get the word out. It's your duty to know them.

Maybe you're the kind of writer who is simply unsure and you jostle through those moments where you can either take it or leave it. Perhaps you find yourself momentarily dipping your toes in the water so to speak. There is certain value in that. "You never step in the same river twice." If it is your curiosity that calls you to write a poem, story, or something genre-less, you're at the best place in the journey. In the tarot deck, the Fool is zero. He's the person with the dog and the knapsack about to step off a cliff if you're looking at the Waite's deck. My teacher, the poet Clayton Eshleman, said to "start with zero as it is both whole and empty." I'm sure he got that from somewhere else.

Regardless of what type of writer you are, you have a voice and something to say. I would add here "a responsibility." You rest (?) on the backs of countless ancestors who resisted in different ways. The very nature of their resistance is/was an act of profound refusal. It was a refusal to accept the narrative of supremacy and the accompanying evil spirits of exploitation, cultural and economic annihilation. The fact that you are indeed here is a testimony to their survival. You've made it this far. Your ability to be who you are is rooted in the sacrifices of your community. This is something that can't be ignored. Remember the "Beautiful Struggle" is an awesome and rewarding responsibility. Read your Audre Lorde! Listen to Jayne Cortez! The question is what are you going to do with that.

What do you see as being your responsibility as a writer? Go look up the countless manifestos, ars poetica, and so on that litter computer and planet. They *are* valuable. They make good reading but what about you and how are you directly informed? I'm writing this in January 2022 and knowing that there are no luxuries to be had unless you buy into a narrative that argues for the benefit of unimpeded greed and exploitation. As someone concerned by art and creation, you must learn to use language, form, sound, movement, and so on to speak not only your voice but the voice of the collective. These are the folks in your community. Always remember that you do not speak for them and indeed there is no "them"; there is no separation. It is not about "you." That's a luxury that ignores our connection to the community of all beings.

I don't know you, but I can tell you with great confidence that your experiences are unique and valuable. I recognize that some of those experiences may have been difficult and that it might be hard to process when you're thinking about making art. At some point, when you're ready, you should consider exploring those places and see what emerges from them. Your imagination is fertile and boundless. Writer Gloria Anzaldúa said that it is the responsibility of the writer to bear witness to what haunts us, to confront the shadow. This is certainly a place where writing can come from.

Then there's the place for joy. Perhaps it's those difficult experiences that define what becomes joyful to you. Sometimes I think that can all be found in the process of writing. You know, getting to those moments when things just seem to flow and their own rhythm. You find yourself in a space where words and phrases and ideas just seem to spring forth out of nowhere. I see it as a kind of alchemy. I'm not sure if you encountered these moments. Write enough and you will. Those moments serve as reminders that writing is beyond the individual self. It brings about the awareness that you are attuned to something greater than you. Check out: Blake, Dickinson, Césaire, Baraka, and so on. This is not new news here. Authentic writing, in my opinion, comes out of study and mystery. I think it's important to know the tradition, *your* tradition. I'm reminded of the word "mixtery," which was coined by a Gullah man who was formally enslaved in South Carolina. That word speaks to me and has become a part of my practice as a writer. I am in a place of wonder when I write.

Writing is not a vocation; it is a practice. How is it a practice for you? My advice is not to seek answers because that implies that you have already formulated a question in your mind. Better to open yourself up to things. There's this great 1970s interview with Ishmael Reed and he's talking about Hoodoo and how it relates to Black creativity. Here's the link: https://www.youtube.com/watch?v=K-BYm0mZnU4

Mix: absorb music, art, dance, comics, chat rooms, and so on. Gain entrance to the rare book room of a library and look through an archive. Go to the laundry mat, the barber shop, the park, learn to listen deeply and translate that depth into words and images. There are wonderful things out there that you need to lay claim to! In the final analysis, it's all about the journey and how you use your voice to connect with others and to bear witness to your time on this planet. That's not really a tall order to fill.

Writing has the advantage to show and convey why we are who we are. Sometimes we as writers don't even see that. That's why it's important to be a writer/reader. That's where the workshop model can be beneficial if it is conducted with compassion. Crucial that you know what's out there. You might also be amazed to know that you will never fully know all that's out there, and that's ok as long as you remain in the process of growth. The workshop can be like an auto body shop. People will tell you how to get your car running properly and that's fine. But what can they tell you if you want your car to fly in the heavens or to be submerged in ocean depths?

Having said all of this, I also know that my advice is not proscriptive as I believe that everybody has their own way. There is also a part of me that will directly tell you that the apparatus of "mystical" thought is just my way of communicating with you. I think that's the beauty of finding your own voice. That it comes out of what is uniquely you. And my hope for you is that your voice be in continual growth and motion. I consider myself to be one of Anansi's children. The lineage of inventiveness and imagination runs through my blood.

T. J. Anderson III is the author of t/here it is (Omnidawn Press, forthcoming Fall 2022), Devonte Travels the Sorry Route (Omnidawn Press, 2019), Cairo Workbook (Willow Books, 2014), River to Cross (The Backwaters Press, 2009), Notes to Make the Sound Come Right: Four Innovators of Jazz Poetry (University of Arkansas Press, 2004), Blood Octave (Flat Five Recordings, 2006), and the chapbook At Last Round Up (lift books, 1996). He has had fellowships with The Virginia Center for the Creative Arts (VCCA) and The MacDowell Colony. He teaches at Hollins University in Roanoke, Virginia.

References

Literary Works

0A Better Life. Dir. Chris Weitz. Lime Orchard Productions, 2011.

A Litany for Survival: The Life and Work of Audre Lorde. Dir. Ada Gay Griffin and Michelle Parkerson. 1995

Abu Hwaij, Oula. "The Benefits of Hijab." *Undergraduate Journal of Gender and Women's Studies* 1.1 (2012) https://escholarship.org/uc/item/4c09451z

Abu Jaber, Diana. *Arabian Jazz*. Harcourt Brace & Company, 1993.

Abu Jaber, Diana. *The Language of Baklava*. Anchor Books, 2005.

Adichie, Chimamanda Ngozi. *Purple Hibiscus*. Algonquin, 2012.

Adnan, Etel. *Sitt Marie Rose*. The Post-Apollo Press, 1982.

Al Abdullah, Queen Rania. *The Sandwich Swap*. Little Brown and Company, 2010.

Amiry, Suad. *Sharon and My Mother-in-Law*. Pantheon Books, 2003.

Amreeka, Dir. Cherien Dabis. Virgil Films, 2009.

Anderson, Celine. "Part One: A Place Without Question." *Dardishi* September 5, 2016a. https://dardishidotcom.wordpress.com/2016/09/05/part-one-a-place-without-question/

Anderson, Celine. "Part Two: A Place Without Question." *Dardishi* September 12, 2016b. https://dardishidotcom.wordpress.com/2016/09/12/part-two-a-place-without-question/

Anderson III, T.J. "An Alphabet for My Daughters." *River to Cross*. The Backwaters Press, 2009a. 93–95.

Anderson III, T.J. "Cairo Workbook." *Cairo Workbook*. Willow Books, 2014. 10–12.

Anderson III, T.J. "the hotel worker." *t/here it is*. Omnidawn, 2022. 52.

Anderson III, T.J. "Same Old Story." *River to Cross*. The Backwaters Press, 2009b. 37.

Anderson, Yasmine. "Meeting." *Mizna: Prose, Poetry, and Art Exploring Arab America* 15.1 (2014): 3.

© The Author(s), under exclusive license to Springer Nature Switzerland AG 2022
P. Kaldas, *Writing the Multicultural Experience*,
https://doi.org/10.1007/978-3-031-06124-0

Anderson, Yasmine. "Yellow." *African American Review* 53.1 (Spring 2020): 55.

Antonia's Line. Dir. Marlene Gorris. Bergen, 1996.

Anzaldúa, Gloria. "How to Tame a Wild Tongue." *Borderlands/La Frontera: The New Mestiza*. Aunt Lute Books, 1987a. 53–64.

Anzaldúa, Gloria. "To Live in the Borderlands Means You." *Borderlands/La Frontera: The New Mestiza*. Aunt Lute Books, 1987b. 194–195.

August, Ashley. "Superstition." *Say I Won't*. Independently Published, 2019. 1.

Balcárcel, Rebecca. *The Other Half of Happy*. Chronicle Books, 2019.

Bruchac, Joseph. *The First Strawberries*. Puffin Books, 1993.

Carved in Silence. Dir. Felicia Lowe. Lowedown Productions, 1987.

Choi, Franny. "To the Man Who Shouted 'I Like Pork Fried Rice' at Me on the Street." *Floating, Brilliant, Gone*. Write Bloody Publishing, 2014. 38–39.

Chrystos. "Today Was a Bad Day Like TB." *Not Vanishing*. Press Gang Publisher, 1989. 17.

Cisneros, Sandra. *Hair/Pelitos*. Alfred A. Knopf, 1994.

Cisneros, Sandra. *The House on Mango Street*. Vintage, 1991.

Cofer, Judith Ortiz. "American History." *The Latin Deli*. Norton, 1993a. 7–15.

Cofer, Judith Ortiz. "And Are You a Latina Writer." *Woman in Front of the Sun*. University of Georgia Press, 2000a. 105–115.

Cofer, Judith Ortiz. *¡A bailar! Let's Dance*. Arte Publico Press, 2011.

Cofer, Judith Ortiz. "The Latin Deli: An Ars Poetica." *The Latin Deli*. Norton, 1993b. 3–4.

Cofer, Judith Ortiz. "My Rosetta." *Woman in Front of the Sun*. The University of Georgia Press, 2000b. 1–18.

Cofer, Judith Ortiz. "The Myth of the Latin Woman: I Just Met A Girl Named Maria." *The Latin Deli*. Norton, 1993c. 148–154.

Cofer, Judith Ortiz. "The Story of My Body." *The Latin Deli*. Norton, 1993d. 135–146.

Craft, Jerry. *New Kid*. Harper, 2019.

Dabaie, Marguerite. *The Hookah Girl and Other True Stories*. Rosarium Publishing, 2018.

Darraj, Susan Muaddi. "How to Plan an Arab Wedding that Will Please Everyone, Inshallah (Except You)." *Middle East Eye*, October 1, 2019. https://www.middleeasteye.net/discover/how-to-plan-arab-wedding

Darraj, Susan Muaddi. "The New World." *Dinarzad's Children: An Anthology of Contemporary Arab American Fiction*. Ed. Pauline Kaldas and Khaled Mattawa. University of Arkansas Press, 2009. 3–18.

De Leon, Jennifer. "Introduction." *Wise Latinas: Writers on Higher Education*. Ed. Jennifer De Leon. University of Nebraska Press, 2014. 1–7.

Diaz, Natalie. "American Arithmetic." *Postcolonial Love Poem*. Graywolf Press, 2020. 17–18.

Double Happiness. Dir. Mina Shum. British Columbia Film Commission, 1995.

Douglas, Marcia. *Madam Fate*. Soho Press, 1999.

Dumas, Firoozeh. "The F Word." *Funny in Farsi*. Random House, 2004a. 62–67.

Dumas, Firoozeh. "Me and Bob Hope." *Funny in Farsi*. Random House, 2004b. 104–110.

Dumas, Firoozeh. "Save Me, Mickey." *Funny in Farsi*. Random House, 2004c. 17–23.

Edgarian, Carol. *Rise the Euphrates*. Random House, 1994.

El Guindi, Yussef. "Stage Directions for an Extended Conversation." *Dinarzad's Children: An Anthology of Contemporary Arab American Fiction*. Ed. Pauline Kaldas and Khaled Mattawa. University of Arkansas Press, 2009. 183–187.

El Rassi, Toufic. *Arab in America*. Last Gasp, 2008.

Engle, Margarita. "Turtle Came to See Me." *Enchanted Air: Two Cultures Two Wings: A Memoir*. Atheneum, 2016. 22.

Esquivel, Laura. *Like Water for Chocolate*. Anchor Books, 1989.

The Farewell. Dir. Lulu Wang. Ray Productions, 2019.

Geha, Joseph. "News from Phoenix." *Dinarzad's Children: An Anthology of Contemporary Arab American Fiction*. Ed. Pauline Kaldas and Khaled Mattawa. University of Arkansas Press, 2009. 83–97.

Gossett, Hattie. "billie lives! billie lives." *This Bridge Called My Back: Writings by Radical Women of Color*. Ed. Cherríe Moraga and Gloria Anzaldúa. Kitchen Table: Women of Color Press, 1981. 109–112.

Gyasi, Yaa. *Homegoing*. Alfred A. Knopf, 2016.

Ha, Robin. *Almost American Girl*. Balzar & Bray, 2020.

Halaby, Laila. *Once in a Promised Land*. Beacon Press, 2008.

Hammad, Suheir. "Exotic." *Born Palestinian, Born Black*. Upset Press, 2010. 64–65.

Harris, Jessica. "In a Leaf of Collard, Green." *We Are What We Ate: 24 Memories of Food*. Ed. Mark Winegardner. Harcourt, 1998. 105–109.

Henríquez, Cristina. *The Book of Unknown Americans*. Vintage, 2015.

Hobson, Brandon. "Escape from the Dysphesiac People." *The Best American Short Stories 2021*. Ed. Jesmyn Ward. Mariner Books, 2021. 53–63.

Howe, Leanne. "Ishki, Mother, Upon Leaving The Choctaw Homelands, 1831." *Famine Pots: The Choctaw–Irish Gift Exchange, 1847–Present*. Eds. Leanne Howe and Padraig Kirwan. Michigan State University Press, 2020. 107–108

Islas, Arturo and Marilyn Yalom. "Interview with Maxine Hong Kingston." *Conversations with Maxine Hong Kingston*. Ed. Paul Skenazy and Tera Martin Jackson. University Press of Mississippi, 1998. 21–32

Jaswal, Balli Kaur. "How a Full Body Wax Helped Me Feel at Home in a New Country" *Cosmopolitan* 22 June 2017. https://www.cosmopolitan.com/style-beauty/beauty/a10042528/full-body-wax-balli-kaur-jaswal/

Jen, Gish. "Don't Ask, Just Eat." *We Are What We Ate: 24 Memories of Food*. Ed. Mark Winegardner. Harcourt, 1998.123–125.

Joukhadar, Zeyn. "Incantations for Unsung Boys" *Columbia Journal* 4 August 2020.

Joukhadar, Zeyn. *The Map of Salt and Stars*. Atria Books, 2019a.

Kahf, Mohja. "Hijab Scene #2." *Emails from Scheherazad*. University Press of Florida, 2003a. 42.

Kahf, Mohja. "Hijab Scene #3." *Emails from Scheherazad*. University Press of Florida, 2003b. 25.

Kahf, Mohja. "Manar of Hama." *Dinarzad's Children: An Anthology of Contemporary Arab American Fiction*. Ed. Pauline Kaldas and Khaled Mattawa. University of Arkansas Press, 2009. 111–117.

Kahf, Mohja. "My Grandmother Washes Her Feet in in the Sink of the Bathroom at Sears." *Emails from Scheherazad*. University Press of Florida, 2003c. 26–28.

Kaldas, Pauline. "ABC/Alif, Beh, Teh." *Egyptian Compass*. Custom Words, 2006a. 15.

Kaldas, Pauline. "Airport." *The Time Between Places*. University of Arkansas Press, 2010a. 101–109.

Kaldas, Pauline. "Cairo Walk." *Egyptian Compass*. Custom Words, 2006b. 60–61.

Kaldas, Pauline. "A Conversation." The Time Between Places. University of Arkansas Press, 2010b. 113–119.

Kaldas, Pauline. "In the Direction of Home." *Home: An Imagined Landscape*. Ed. Marjorie Agosín. Solis Press, 2016. 1–14.

Kaldas, Pauline. *Letters from Cairo*. Syracuse University Press, 2007.

Kaldas, Pauline. "Name: An Improvisation on Sound." *Looking Both Ways*. Cune Books, 2017a. 13–19.

Kaldas, Pauline. "To Walk Cautiously in the World." *Looking Both Ways*. Cune Books, 2017b. 89–92.

Khan-Cullors, Patrisse. "Community Interrupted." *When They Call You a Terrorist: A Black Lives Matter Memoir* St. Martins, 2020. 9–17.

Kim, Myung Mi. "Into Such Assembly." *Under Flag*. Kelsey St. Press, 1991. 29–31.

Kingston, Maxine Hong. *The Woman Warrior*. Vintage, 1975.

Kiyama, Henry (Yoshitaka). *The Four Immigrant Manga*. Stone Bridge Press, 1999.

Lahiri, Jhumpa. *The Namesake*. Houghton Mifflin, 2003.

Lai, Him Mark, Genny Lim, and Judy Yung. *Island: Poetry & History of Chinese Immigrants on Angel Island, 1910–1940*, 2nd edition. University of Washington Press, 2014.

Laméris, Danusha. "Insha'Allah." *The Moons of August*. Autumn House Press, 2014. 19

Lorde, Audre. "Power." *The Collected Poems of Audre Lorde*. Norton, 2000. 319–320.

The Lunchbox. Dir. Ritesh Batra. Sikhya Entertainment, 2013.

Majaj, Lisa Suhair. "Cadence." *Geographies of Light*. Del Sol Press, 2009a. 65–66.

Majaj, Lisa Suhair. "Fifty Years On/Stones in an Unfinished Wall." *Geographies of Light*. Del Sol Press, 2009b. 88–96.

Majaj, Lisa Suhair. "Origins." *Geographies of Light*. Del Sol Press, 2009c. 14.

Majaj, Lisa Suhair. "Recognized Futures." *Geographies of Light*. Del Sol Press, 2009d. 63–64.

Majaj, Lisa Suhair. "These Words." *Geographies of Light*. Del Sol Press, 2009e. 98–99.

Mattawa, Khaled. "First Snow." *Dinarzad's Children: An Anthology of Contemporary Arab American Fiction*. Ed. Pauline Kaldas and Khaled Mattawa. University of Arkansas Press, 2009. 357–365.

Mattawa, Khaled. "Repatriation: A Libya Memoir." *Beyond Memory: An Anthology of Arab American Creative Nonfiction*. Ed. Pauline Kaldas and Khaled Mattawa. University of Arkansas Press, 2020. 173–184.

Mattawa, Khaled. "Zai El-Hawa." *Ismailia Eclipse*. The Sheep Meadow Press, 1995. 60–61.

Mbue, Imbolo. *Behold the Dreamers*. Random House, 2016.

Mersal, Iman. "Displaced." *Beyond Memory: An Anthology of Arab American Creative Nonfiction*. Ed. Pauline Kaldas and Khaled Mattawa. University of Arkansas Press, 2020. 185–190.

Nelson, Marilyn. "Emmet Till's Name Still Catches in My Throat." *Resisting Arrest: Poems to Stretch the Sky*. Ed. Tony Medina. Jacar Press, 2016. 68.

Ng, Celeste. *Everything I Never Told You*. Penguin, 2014.

Nye, Naomi Shihab. "My Father and the Figtree." *Words Under the Words*. Far Corner Books, 1980. 20–21.

Nye, Naomi Shihab. "One Village" *Beyond Memory: An Anthology of Arab American Creative Nonfiction*. Ed. Pauline Kaldas and Khaled Mattawa. University of Arkansas Press, 2020. 215–231.

Nye, Naomi Shihab. *Sitti's Secrets*. Aladdin Books, 1997.

Ousmane, Sembene. *God's Bits of Wood*. Heinemann, 1962.

Pham, Andrew X. *Catfish and Mandala*. Farrar, Straus and Giroux, 1999.

Philip, M. Nourbese. "The Declension of History in the Key of If." *Letters to the Future: Black Women Radical Writing*. Ed. Erica Hunt and Dawn Lundy Martine. Kore Press, 2018. 297–317.

Philip, M. Nourbese. *Zong*. Wesleyan University Press, 2011.

Rushin, Donna Kate. "The Bridge Poem." *This Bridge Called My Back: Writings by Radical Women of Color*. Ed. Cherrie Moraga and Gloria Anzaldúa. Kitchen Table: Women of Color Press, 1981. xxi–xxii.

Ryan, Pam Muñoz. *Esperanza Rising*. Scholastic, 2016.

Senna, Danzy. *Caucasia*. Riverhead Books, 1999.

Sweet Land. Dir. Ali Selim. Libero LLC, 2006.

Tan, Amy. "Confessions." *Short Takes: Brief Encounters with Contemporary Nonfiction*. Ed. Judith Kitchen, 2005. 88–90.

Tan, Amy, "Mother Tongue." *Touchstone Anthology of Contemporary Creative Nonfiction*. Ed. Lex Williford and Michael Martone. Simon & Schuster, 2007. 514–519.

Uchida, Yoshiko. *Desert Exile*. University of Washington Press, 1982.

The Visitor. Dir. Thomas McCarthy. Groundswell Productions, 2008.

Wadjda. Dir. Haifaa Al-Mansour. Razor Film Produktion GmbH, 2013.

Woo, Merle. "Letter to Ma." *This Bridge Called My Back: Writings by Radical Women of Color*. Eds. Cherríe Moraga and Gloria Anzaldúa. SUNY Press, 2015. 138–145.

Yoon, Nicola. *The Sun is Also a Star*. Random House, 2016.

Yunis, Alia. "The Lebanon-Detroit Express" in *Dinarzad's Children: An Anthology of Contemporary Arab American Fiction*. Ed. Pauline Kaldas and Khaled Mattawa. University of Arkansas Press, 2009. 375–378.

Zitkala-Sa. *American Indian Stories*. University of Nebraska Press, 1921.

Works Cited

Adichie, Chimamanda Ngozi. "The Power of a Single Story." *YouTube*. 18 April 2016.

Chavez, Felicia Rose. *The Anti-Racist Writing Workshop: How to Decolonize the Creative Classroom*. Haymarket Books, 2021.

Cofer, Judith Ortiz. "5:00 AM: Writing as Ritual." *The Latin Deli*. Norton, 1993e. 166–168.

Cofer, Judith Ortiz. "But Tell it Slant: From Poetry to Prose and Back Again." *Writing Creative Nonfiction*. Ed. Carolyn Forché and Philip Gerard. Story Press, 2001. 8–13.

Cofer, Judith Ortiz. "The Woman Who Slept with One Eye Open." *Woman in Front of the Sun*. University of Georgia Press, 2000c. 73–90.

D'Aguiar, Fred. "Toward A New Creative Writing Pedagogy." *The Writer's Chronicle* 49.2 (October/November 2016): 84–95.

DeLeon, Jennifer. "Ethnicity and Craft." *Poets & Writers* (Jan-Feb 2015) 31–35.

Diaz, Junot. "MFA vs. POC." *The New Yorker* 30 April 2014.

Falcón, Kandace Creel. "What Would Eden Say? Reclaiming the Personal and Grounding Story in Chicana Feminist (Academic) Writing." *How Dare We! Write: A Multicultural Creative Writing Discourse*. Ed. Sherry Quan Lee. Modern History Press, 2017. 8–15.

Hallman, J.C., ed. *The Story about the Story*. Tin House Books, 2009.

Hallman, J.C., ed. *The Story about the Story II*. Tin House Books, 2013.

Joukhadar, Zeyn. "Love Letters to Those Who Came Before Me." *Shenandoah* 68.2 (2019b). https://shenandoahliterary.org/682/excerpt/

Lee, Sherry Quan, ed. *How Dare We! Write: A Multicultural Creative Writing Discourse*. Modern History Press, 2017.

Lyman, Jessica Lopez. "Imposter Poet: Recovering from Graduate School." *How Dare We! Write: A Multicultural Creative Writing Discourse*. Ed. Sherry Quan Lee. Modern History Press, 2017. 16–21.

Miller, Brenda: "A Braided Heart: Shaping the Lyric Essay." *Writing Creative Nonfiction*. Ed. Carolyn Forché and Philip Gerard. Story Press, 2001. 14–24.

Moore, Dinty. "The Comfortable Chair: Using Humor in Creative Nonfiction." *Writing Creative Nonfiction*. Ed. Carolyn Forché and Philip Gerard. Story Press, 2001. 122–129.

Mura, David. "Ferguson, Whiteness as Default and the Teaching of Creative Writing." *The Writer's Chronicle* 49.2 (October/November 2016): 34–44.

Mura, David. *A Stranger's Journey: Race, Identity, and Narrative Craft in Writing*. The University of Georgia Press, 2018.

Rankin, Claudia. "In Our Way: Racism in Creative Writing." *The Writer's Chronicle* 49.2 (October/November 2016): 46–58.

Rendon, Marcie. "Creating Native American Mirrors: and Making a Living as a Writer." *How Dare We! Write: A Multicultural Creative Writing Discourse*. Ed. Sherry Quan Lee. Modern History Press, 2017. 89–95.

Takaki, George. *Iron Cages: Race and Culture in 19th Century America*. Oxford University Press, 2000.

Index

CPSIA information can be obtained
at www.ICGtesting.com
Printed in the USA
LVHW021003140523
746947LV00004B/313